NEW DIRECTIONS FOR TEACHING AND LEARNING

Robert J. Menges, *Northwestern University*
EDITOR-IN-CHIEF

Marilla D. Svinicki, *University of Texas, Austin*
ASSOCIATE EDITOR

Building a Diverse Faculty

Joanne Gainen
Santa Clara University

Robert Boice
State University of New York at Stony Brook

EDITORS

Number 53, Spring 1993

JOSSEY-BASS PUBLISHERS
San Francisco

BUILDING A DIVERSE FACULTY
Joanne Gainen, Robert Boice (eds.)
New Directions for Teaching and Learning, no. 53
Robert J. Menges, Editor-in-Chief
Marilla D. Svinicki, Associate Editor

Microfilm copies of issues and articles are available in 16mm and 35mm,
as well as microfiche in 105mm, through University Microfilms Inc., 300
North Zeeb Road, Ann Arbor, Michigan 48106.

LC 85-644763   ISSN 0271-0633   ISBN 1-55542-725-1

NEW DIRECTIONS FOR TEACHING AND LEARNING is part of The Jossey-Bass
Higher and Adult Education Series and is published quarterly by Jossey-
Bass Inc., Publishers, 350 Sansome Street, San Francisco, California
94104-1310. Second-class postage paid at San Francisco, California, and at
additional mailing offices. POSTMASTER: Send address changes to New
Directions for Teaching and Learning, Jossey-Bass Inc., Publishers, 350
Sansome Street, San Francisco, California 94104-1310.

SUBSCRIPTIONS for 1993 cost $45.00 for individuals and $60.00 for institutions, agencies, and libraries.

EDITORIAL CORRESPONDENCE should be sent to Robert J. Menges, Northwestern University, Center for the Teaching Professions, 2003 Sheridan
Road, Evanston, Illinois 60208-2610.

Cover photograph by Richard Blair/Color & Light   © 1990.

The paper used in this journal is acid-free and meets the strictest
guidelines in the United States for recycled paper (50 percent
recycled waste, including 10 percent post-consumer waste).
Manufactured in the United States of America.

CONTENTS

Editors' Notes

Perhaps the most visible trend in higher education today is the increasing diversity of our students. Their presence on campus might lead us to expect a corresponding trend toward greater diversity among the faculty. Instead, we find a disturbing flatness in the faculty curve: while the overall numbers of women and minorities have in fact increased, their presence as a percentage of the faculty has not kept pace with their growing numbers in the population as a whole nor with their increased presence at the undergraduate level. Moreover, women and minorities among the faculty find the climate less than welcoming. Their scholarship is frequently undervalued, they receive less mentoring than their more traditional peers, and the fierce debate over "multiculturalism" in the curriculum reveals the academy's ambivalence about the presence of their ideas and values within the ivy walls.

Because most administrators and senior faculty are neither women nor minorities, they may be unaware of the ways in which their institutions inadvertently create an inhospitable climate for nontraditional faculty. Working from the premise that we must openly address our discomfort about issues of race, gender, and sexual orientation, *Building a Diverse Faculty* seeks to heighten awareness about the experiences that facilitate or obstruct academic careers for diverse people. The collection proceeds from an overview of the literature on faculty diversity to close-up accounts and statistical reports on specific faculty groups. Throughout, the authors point out ways institutions can act to ensure the continued presence and success of faculty who do not fit the traditional academic profile.

In Chapter One, Linda K. Johnsrud reviews the literature on women and minority faculty, and offers propositions to guide policymaking and practice. Chapter Two, by Phyllis Bronstein, Esther D. Rothblum, and Sondra E. Solomon, distinguishes three forms of barriers: institutional, social, and psychological; their work complements Johnsrud's demographic portrayal by portraying sources of discouragement experienced by women and minority graduate students and faculty. Chapter Three, by Hisauro Garza, describes the significant underrepresentation of the Chicano/Latino population among the faculty and documents their sense of second-class citizenship in the academic world. William G. Tierney and Robert A. Rhoads, reporting in Chapter Four on the struggles of gay, lesbian, and bisexual faculty, argue that leaders must speak out clearly and positively to support "communities of difference," especially in response to homophobic attacks.

Chapter Five challenges the myth that Asian Pacific Americans have few "minority" problems in higher education, citing evidence of discrimination based on distribution data and specific tenure cases, including that of the author, Don T. Nakanishi. A theme running through all these accounts is that scholarship on a particular group, especially if conducted by a member of that group, is undervalued. This theme permeates Chapter Six, in which Phyllis Bronstein reveals the struggles for legitimacy of a group of scholars engaged in research on sociocultural and gender issues in psychology.

Turning toward possible sources of improvement in this bleak situation, Chapter Seven, by Robert Boice, identifies early—and seemingly irreversible—turning points that sabotage the careers of women and minority faculty, and describes strategies to prevent the occurrence of such events and subsequent early derailment of otherwise promising academic careers.

Another theme, early discouragement and lack of mentoring, is addressed by a major, national, federally funded program designed to encourage African American and other minority students to pursue careers in science; in Chapter Eight, Robert M. Hoyte and Jonathan Collett describe faculty involvement in that program. In Chapter Nine, Joanne Gainen describes a more modest but cost-effective and readily reproducible program to counteract the lack of mentoring experienced by many women and minority faculty: a writing support group that draws on research-based strategies to enhance scholarly productivity. We conclude in Chapter Ten with a brief synthesis of issues raised and directions suggested by this diverse group of authors.

Affirmative action may (arguably) help to bring more women and minorities into the academy; but only faculty and administrators already in the academy can provide the resources, information, and support that will make these newcomers an integral part of institutional life. We believe this volume will provide useful guidance for those who want to see the promise of educational access translated into the reality of an intellectually vigorous, caring, and diverse academic community.

Joanne Gainen
Robert Boice
Editors

JOANNE GAINEN (formerly Joanne Kurfiss) is director of the Teaching and Learning Center and an associate dean in the College of Arts and Sciences, Santa Clara University. She is author of Critical Thinking: Theory, Research, Practice, and Possibilities.

ROBERT BOICE is professor of psychology and director of the Faculty Instructional Support Office at the State University of New York at Stony Brook. He is author of The New Faculty Member.

Women and minorities become scarcer as one climbs the ladder of institutional prestige; and their career paths, salaries, work loads, departure rates, and feelings of integration differ markedly from those of white males.

Women and Minority Faculty Experiences: Defining and Responding to Diverse Realities

Linda K. Johnsrud

Reviewing the literature on women and ethnic and racial minority[1] faculty is a more daunting task today than it was even ten years ago. Underrepresented groups that once received virtually no attention are now subject to widespread scrutiny. Projected faculty shortages, increased attrition and retirements, and commitments to enhancing diversity in the face of shrinking candidate pools have combined to lend urgency to recruiting and retaining women and minority faculty. Concomitantly, the literature aimed at understanding the issues and barriers faced by women and minority faculty has burgeoned.

Although the literature is rich and growing, it is diverse in purpose (conceptual, empirical, and programmatic), method (qualitative and quantitative), design (case studies and national surveys), and orientation (individual coping and organizational change). Moreover, the faculty studied differ by career stage (new and experienced, tenured and nontenured), institutional type (research and comprehensive university, liberal arts college, and community college), and level of disaggregation (women only, African American only, non-White collectively). Categorizations of ethnic and minority group members are not consistent in the literature. For example, African Americans may be subsumed in the "Black" category, Chicanos in the Hispanic, and American Indian in the Native American. Persons of Puerto Rican, Cuban, and Dominican descent may be included in either (or both) Black and Hispanic categories. Foreign-born and native-born distinctions are rarely made.

The purpose of this review is to identify the commonalities that emerge regarding the experiences of women and ethnic minority faculty. Individual campuses would be well served to examine their own unique context and the experiences of their women and minority faculty members. The reality is, however, that the numbers of women and minority faculty on individual campuses are low, and as a result confidentiality is often an issue in attempting to disaggregate and report the findings. Thus, this review is offered as a template that institutions can use as a starting point. The broad question that guided the review is, "How can the current literature inform the efforts of colleges and universities in enabling the success of a diverse faculty?"

This chapter begins with an overview of the demographics of women and ethnic faculty. Next, their perceptions of their experiences within the academy are described. Finally, three propositions are offered for institutions striving to enhance and support a diverse faculty.

Demographic Realities

In 1986 women received 35 percent of all doctoral degrees awarded, reflecting a steady increase from 13 percent in 1970 (Touchton and Davis, 1991). And yet, of the 489,000 full-time instructional faculty in 1987, 73 percent were men and 27 percent were women (National Center for Education Statistics, 1991). This proportion has not changed since 1981–1982 (Bowen and Schuster, 1986). Longitudinal data indicate that the proportions of women and men with tenure status have also remained virtually the same during the past decade. In 1980–1981 only 49.7 percent of women faculty were tenured, compared to 70.0 percent of the men, while in 1989–1990 48.5 percent were tenured, compared to 69.7 percent of the male faculty (National Center for Education Statistics, 1991). The distribution of women in ranks and by institutional type is also skewed. That is, women faculty are proportionately better represented in community colleges and liberal arts colleges than in research universities, and women are clustered in the lower ranks (Touchton and Davis, 1991). If progress continues at the same rate it has since 1975, it will take women ninety years to be equally represented in the academic ranks of doctoral-granting institutions (Alpert, 1989). In an effort to discover "where women professors are in the USA," Farley (1990) notes that women comprise only 18 percent of the total faculty at Ivy League and Big Ten institutions. She comments, "the more prestigious the institution, the fewer the women on the faculty" (p. 199).

The demographic realities for faculty from minority ethnic and racial groups are even more disturbing. Of the 489,000 full-time instructional faculty in 1987, 89.5 percent were White, 3.2 percent were Black, 2.3 percent were Hispanic, 4.2 percent were Asian, and 0.7 percent were American

Indian (National Center for Education Statistics, 1991). This total of 10.4 percent minority faculty represents a slight increase over the 7.2 percent reported in 1976 (Bowen and Schuster, 1986, p. 58). Moreover, the minority candidate pools have not improved numerically since 1987 ("Earned Degrees, 1989–90"), despite the growth of the minority population. Census data indicate that 12.1 percent of the population is Black (U.S. Bureau of the Census, 1991), but only 4.0 percent of the doctoral degrees awarded in 1989–1990 went to Blacks; Hispanics are similarly underrepresented, receiving only 2.7 percent of the doctorates while making up 9.0 percent of the population. Asians are somewhat overrepresented, receiving 4.4 percent of the doctorates although they comprise only 2.9 percent of the population. American Indians received 0.3 percent of the doctorates while census data indicate that 0.8 percent of the population is Native American.

Most data treat minority faculty members as one group; as a result, the situation of non-White women is often obscured. The proportion of women faculty who are minorities remained stable between 1975 and 1985 at 12 percent (Touchton and Davis, 1991). In 1985 7 percent of the tenured women faculty were Black, 2 percent were Hispanic, 3 percent were Asian, and less than 1 percent were American Indian. Furthermore, the candidate pool does not hold promise for the future. Of the 12,196 doctoral degrees awarded to women (excluding nonresident aliens) in 1989–1990, 87.7 percent were awarded to White women, 5.0 percent were awarded to Black women, 3.0 percent were awarded to Hispanic women, 3.1 percent were awarded to Asian women, and 0.4 percent were awarded to American Indian women ("Earned Degrees, 1989–90"). The percentages of non-White men receiving doctorates relative to White men are even lower (with the exception of Asian men). These proportions indicate that recruitment of ethnic and racial minorities will remain a challenge for colleges and universities in the future. The need for enhanced recruitment efforts has been developed elsewhere (see, for example, Justiz, Bjork, and Wilson, 1988); the focus of this review is on retaining and advancing those who have been recruited into faculty positions.

Conflicting Realities Between Women and Men, Minorities and Nonminorities

The research on women and minority faculty reveals one striking pattern: women and minority faculty experience the academy differently than their male counterparts. The notion that White men enjoy an advantaged career path into and through the academy pervades the literature. In the early eighties language emerged describing the "accumulation of advantages and disadvantages" by young scientists (Cole, 1979; Smelser and Content, 1980). Later Clark and Corcoran (1986, p. 20) spoke directly to the "accumulative disadvantage" of women academics that begins in graduate school and grows with time. Similarly, Exum (1983, p. 394) describes the minority faculty experience as a "succession of exclusions" occurring at each stage of the faculty career. The experiences of women and minorities who have held or are holding faculty positions are described in the following sections.

Women Faculty Members' Experience in the Academy. The most blatant disparity between the experience of women and men faculty may be in salary. Salary inequities have been documented across all academic ranks (Touchton and Davis, 1991). In a recent analysis using national data from full-time faculty at four-year colleges and universities, Smart (1991) found that gender is more important to both faculty members' academic rank and salary than the type of institution in which they work, their academic discipline, or the nature of the work they perform. Moreover, women do not receive the same returns (salary, promotion, upward mobility, research monies, and so forth) for their research productivity that men do for theirs (Ervin, Thomas, and Zey-Ferrell, 1984; Persell, 1983).

Disparities also exist in the workload women faculty carry. They spend less time in research-related activities and more in teaching (Armour, Fuhrmann, and Wergin, 1990; Finkelstein, 1984; Davis and Astin, 1990; Russell, 1991), and more time in service to the university (Carnegie Foundation for the Advancement of Teaching, 1990). These differences may vary by institutional type. For example, evidence suggests that women in research universities spend the same amount of time on research that men do, and moreover that they hold the same goals and interests regarding research and teaching that their male counterparts hold (Sorcinelli and Andrews, 1987; Olsen, Maple, and Stage, 1991).

Findings on the relative productivity of women and men faculty are mixed. Some evidence suggests that women have lower levels of research performance (Cole, 1979; Russell, 1991); some indicates that men exceed the output of women in quantity but not quality (Persell, 1983); and other evidence indicates that there is no difference by gender in productivity (Davis and Astin, 1990; McElrath, 1992). Whatever the reality, data do indicate that women tend to be promoted and tenured more slowly than male faculty, and they are more likely to leave an institution prior to going up for tenure (Finkelstein, 1984; Johnsrud and Atwater, 1991; Rausch, Ortiz, Douthitt, and Reed, 1989).

The fact that women faculty leave in greater proportions than men is not surprising. Women's perceptions of the academic environment are strikingly different from those of their male peers. Feelings of isolation, loneliness, and disconnectedness are well documented (Bourguignon and others, 1987; Johnsrud and Atwater, 1991; Olsen, Maple, and Stage, 1991; Yoder, 1985). Given the low numbers of women in faculty positions, many individual women are the first or the only women in their departments. Women are not as well integrated into departmental or institutional networks

(Eveslage, Stonewater, and Dingerson, 1987; Kaufman, 1978), and perhaps as a result they look more to national networks for professional support (Parson, Sands, and Duane, 1992). At the same time, they do not seem to have the same access to professional networks as men do (O'Leary and Mitchell, 1990; Moore and Sagaria, 1991). O'Leary and Mitchell contend that high levels of integration lead to high levels of visibility, and consequently can have high payoffs in productivity for men. Women, who tend to be on the periphery, cannot capitalize on this source of career support to the same degree that men can.

Women also describe their need to carefully monitor their style and tone of communicating to avoid being labeled either too passive or too aggressive (Bourguignon and others, 1987); they report more difficulties in relationships with departmental chairs and colleagues (Johnsrud and Atwater, 1991); and they describe themselves as "outsiders," feeling that they do not belong (Aisenberg and Harrington, 1988). The majority of women faculty at one public university felt that their work was undervalued because of their sex (Parsons, Sands, and Duane, 1991). Other women have reported that their scholarship is trivialized and discredited (Kritek, 1984). The collective perceptions and experiences of the women faculty described here suggest that women feel like "misfits" (Reynolds, 1989, p. 7) and that they are treated as if they do not belong when they pursue academic careers.

Minority Faculty Members' Experience in the Academy. The experience of minority faculty parallels in many respects the experiences of women but with some important differences. Although the research on minority group members is limited, there is growing evidence that they experience severe marginalization (Boice, in press; Bourguignon and others, 1987). They cite everyday interactions, both social and professional, as sources of their feeling unwelcomed, unappreciated, and unwanted. They perceive that colleagues assume they were hired for affirmative action purposes; thus they feel pressured to continually prove that they deserve their positions (Menges and Exum, 1983; Luz Reyes and Halcon, 1988). They feel a need to work harder than White males to win their respect and to gain access to research facilities and funding (Bourguignon and others, 1987). In a study of senior faculty (Armour, Fuhrmann, and Wergin, 1990), minority faculty were twice as likely as their White colleagues to be making plans to leave their current institutions, and they were more likely to believe they have a good chance of moving to a different career.

Minority faculty whose scholarship focuses on ethnic issues express tremendous concern over having their work devalued and dismissed as out of the mainstream or self-serving (Bourguignon and others, 1987; Garza, this volume; Luz Reyes and Halcon, 1988). Some feel that they must cultivate a scholarly interest that is acceptable for publication in "White" journals. Also their scholarly work, as well as their community involvement, is often oriented toward social change which is devalued as nonacademic and questioned as to its appropriateness (Banks, 1984; Bourguignon and others, 1987).

In a major national study of minority Ph.D.'s supported by Educational Testing Service and the Graduate Record Examinations Board, Brown (1988) concluded that the problem of underrepresentation of minority faculty is a problem of supply, flow into and through the academic pipeline, and minority retention. This study indicated that Black Ph.D.'s had the "most fragile status of all minorities and their participation in academe is, at best, marginal" (p. 25). For example, longitudinal data revealed that Black Ph.D.'s had the lowest promotion and tenure rates among minority groups, and except for promotions to associate professor rank, their rates were consistently below the national average.

Studies of productivity of minority scholars are rare. One study matched eighty-one Black faculty with ninety-two White faculty in the Big Ten universities and found no racial differences in scholarly productivity (Elmore and Blackburn, 1983). More recently, using a national data set, Russell (1991) reports the same finding: no difference in productivity between minorities and nonminorities.

The ETS/GRE study also provided information about the primary work activities of minority faculty (Brown, 1988). Blacks indicated that their primary activity was teaching, followed by administration, with research third. Hispanics listed teaching first, followed by research, then administration. Only Asian Americans listed research first, followed by teaching, then administration. This orientation may account for the promotion and tenure rates of Asian Americans which, although lower than the national average, are higher than those of other minority groups.

Minorities face a number of barriers in the tenure review process. They tend to hold more split or joint appointments (Menges and Exum, 1983); they often value teaching and service which is less likely to be recognized or rewarded; and, as noted above, they spend more time on these activities as well as on student advising (Banks, 1984; McEvans and Applebaum, 1992; Menges and Exum, 1983). Minority faculty members are often less familiar with the politics and unwritten rules governing the academy (Bourguignon and others, 1987), perhaps because they are often isolated and without mentors (Boice, in press). As compared to their White peers, minority faculty perceive more pressure regarding tenure; feel their graduate preparation for the faculty role is more of a problem in their individual development; and perceive that their visibility as a minority erodes their autonomy (Johnsrud and Atwater, 1992). Lack of knowledge regarding the criteria for tenure and promotion, lack of collegial support, and the subjective aspects of the process are also cited as barriers to their advancement (Exum, Menges, Watkins, and Berglund, 1984).

Finally, racism and discrimination are realities in the experience of ethnic and racial minority faculty (Banks, 1984; Bourguignon and others, 1987). Luz Reyes and Halcon (1988) eloquently describe the racism experienced by Chicano faculty in the academy. They document both overt racism (for example, a comment from a dean regarding several Chicano candidates for faculty positions: "What do they think this is, Taco University?" [p. 302]) and covert racism, including tokenism (for example, reducing minority-occupied positions to subordinate status), typecasting (specialized hiring for minority slots), and the taboo against "brown-on-brown" research (the devaluing of research by minorities regarding their minority status and experience).

Clearly, ethnic and racial minority faculty experience the academy differently than their White counterparts. Despite the relative lack of research on minority faculty concerns, it is evident from the literature cited here that the reality of the faculty experience for minorities is often negative, and the problems seem to be pervasive.

Responding to Diverse Realities

As the foregoing descriptions demonstrate, colleges and universities have not been receptive to women and minority faculty. The issues and barriers that women and minority faculty face will not be easily eradicated. Some are a matter of policy, some of practice, and still others are a matter of personal attitudes and human relations. These issues demand response at every level of the academic organization: at the institutional level, within colleges and departments, and at the individual level. Institutions genuinely interested in retaining these diverse faculty and enabling their success must attend to their realities. The following broad propositions are drawn from the literature and intended to guide institutional efforts:

PROPOSITION 1. *Institutions must ensure that the appropriate supports and incentives for research, service, and teaching are available and accessible to women and minority faculty.*

Women and minority faculty do not enter their academic positions with the same support, knowledge, or political savvy that many of their White male peers have. Sponsorship from advisers has been identified as a vital ingredient in the most successful faculty careers (Corcoran and Clark, 1984). Institutions must recognize that not only do women and minority faculty start from behind, but also they often run the race with a sandbag on one shoulder—and that burden is the reality of their sex and their race. As I noted above, their minority status results in extra demands. They are showcased on committees, they are sought after by students, and particularly in the case of ethnic and racial minorities, they are symbols for their communities which they feel obligated to serve (Exum, 1983; Banks, 1984). Many institutions want their faculty to serve in these extraordinary ways; if so, they must include such activities in the reward structure and ensure that women and minorities are not penalized for their contributions. Teaching, working with students, and engaging in service activities are highly valued by many women and minority faculty but when the time demands of their teaching, advising, and committee assignments are unfair, these faculty feel misused, and their scholarly productivity is inhibited (Bourguignon and others, 1987; Davis and Astin, 1990).

The ambiguity of tenure and promotion criteria is legendary; for groups who experience the academy as "outsiders," the lack of clarity in performance norms can result in failure. Institutions must require departments to clarify their requirements for tenure and promotion, communicate them broadly, and provide the supports necessary for success. Women and minorities require the same resources that their White male peers require: adequate facilities for research, graduate student assistance, access to internal and extramural funding, computing and clerical support. Women and minorities, however, report that they must work harder to gain such support and access (Bourguignon and others, 1987). Highly productive women faculty underscore the role that a supportive institutional environment plays in their success (Davis and Astin, 1990). Consequently, institutions must ensure parity in resource allocation. Merit is assumed to operate in competitions for scarce resources but patronage and sponsorship are realities that must be acknowledged. If women and minorities reside on the periphery of the academy, they are far less likely to receive the same assistance as those on the "inside."

Institutional policies regarding childbearing leave, parenting leave, part-time tenure, and the tenure clock should be examined, acknowledging that family issues can result in significant sources of stress and overload for women faculty, and to a lesser degree, for men faculty. A recent study (Teevan, Pepper, and Pellizzari, 1992) indicated that given the responses from both women and men, accommodation of family and career is not solely a women's issue among academics. Nonetheless, there is abundant evidence that these matters are of critical concern to women because of their professional consequences (Austin and Pilat, 1990; Bourguignon and others, 1987; Hensel, 1991; Montgomery, 1989; Sorcinelli and Near, 1989).

PROPOSITION 2. *Institutions must create structures that enable department chairs and senior faculty to facilitate the success of women and minority faculty.*

Poor relationships with department chairs and colleagues are often cited as extremely detrimental to morale and achievement by faculty who leave their positions, particularly women (Johnsrud and Atwater, 1991). Turner and Boice (1989) found that new faculty who judged their chairs as incompetent or unsupportive were highly demoralized and unhappy. The role of the chair is central to a number of concerns, including a sense of belonging, career progress and support, and equity in resources. Institutions must articulate the role of the department chair in supporting and developing the talent of faculty, especially that of women and minorities. Department chairs too often expect faculty to "hit the ground running" (Whitt, 1991). Rather, they should actively identify the strengths and weaknesses, needs and expectations of their faculty, and do what they can to facilitate their growth and advancement. Women and minorities may, however, doubt the motives of those offering assistance (Boice, in press). Despite the traditional norm of autonomy that many faculty cherish, an adept chair can make offers of assistance and support a matter of course, assess the extent to which help is welcomed, and act accordingly.

The selection of chairs should be monitored by deans and ongoing training instituted. Training should include attention to issues of professional work climate, staff training and development, sexual and racial harassment, and affirmative action. All department chairs and department personnel committee chairs should be trained to provide timely, thorough, and constructive performance reviews to tenure-track faculty. Annual reviews ought to explicitly address progress toward tenure; using departmental criteria, chairs should make concrete recommendations to increase the candidate's chances for a positive tenure decision. Chairs and departmental personnel committees should monitor carefully the progress of tenure-track faculty, and, when appropriate, encourage them to pursue tenure early. Early tenure can serve to retain faculty. The granting of tenure demonstrates departmental and institutional commitment to faculty members and relieves their pervading sense of anxiety (Johnsrud and Atwater, 1991).

Many women and minority faculty could gain immeasurably from increased interaction with senior colleagues. Campuses that have instituted formal mentoring relationships between junior and senior faculty have reported high levels of satisfaction on the part of both sets of participants (Boice, 1990; Wunsch and Johnsrud, 1992). Even without formal programs, interaction and collaboration can be encouraged. One of the most disappointing aspects of academic life for new faculty is the lack of collegiality and collaborative spirit which women and minority faculty seem to feel most acutely (Bourguignon and others, 1987; Johnsrud and Atwater, 1991; Reynolds, 1989; Sorcinelli and Andrews, 1987). Collaborative research or teaching can be encouraged by deliberately earmarking monies for joint efforts. Social and intellectual interaction within the department and college can be enhanced in other ways. For example, Ferren (1989) describes in detail one college's successful effort in instituting an annual faculty colloquium that invigorates participants and markedly improves the sense of academic collegiality. One demographic reality of recently hired women and minority faculty is that they tend to be more recently trained than the majority of their colleagues. Efforts such as colloquia and collaborative projects might lessen the generation gap—bridging the differences in training and research orientation that contribute to the sense of isolation for many faculty.

PROPOSITION 3. *Institutions must attend to the climate of their campuses and create a culture that honors gender and ethnic diversity.*

Although many of the foregoing suggestions would enhance the campus climate for women and minority faculty, what is needed is a genuine commitment to end discrimination and racism no matter how covert, and to actively honor gender and ethnic diversity. Presidents and other campus leaders must address these issues with conviction. It should be clear to all members of the campus community that racial or sexual harassment will not be tolerated. Policies should be clear, well publicized, and strictly enforced.

Furthermore, campus leaders at all levels must set a tone that challenges faculty to strive for a diverse community built on mutual respect and a commitment to creating an exemplary educational environment. For example, chairs are in key positions to recognize and eliminate disparate treatment at the departmental level. Women and minorities are dependent upon the chair's awareness and intervention to ensure a positive working environment conducive to their retention and advancement. That sexism and racism are increasingly covert requires that all faculty must be vigilant in their efforts to welcome and support women and minority faculty.

The language used by many women and minority faculty clearly indicts the present climate. Marginalized, isolated, discounted, confused, undervalued, patronized, trivialized—all connote an experience that is at worst hostile, at best devoid of common courtesy. It is important to note that studies of job satisfaction indicate that women and minority faculty often express overall levels of job satisfaction comparable to White males (Armour, Fuhrmann, and Wergin, 1990; Olsen, Maple, and Stage, 1991). Nonetheless, they describe their experiences—and the sources of their satisfaction and dissatisfaction—very differently from White males. The need for a more humane and accepting climate in the academy is evident in much of what they report.

A primary avenue for enhancing understanding and appreciation between colleagues may be through scholarly exchanges. Colloquia, workshops, seminars, and curriculum development opportunities can be scheduled to introduce the "new" scholarship by women and minority faculty. This work might be valued more if its critics understood it more thoroughly. In addition, work that focuses on the realities of female and ethnic experiences can inform those that are male and/or White. Much of the distance and disconnectedness felt by women and minority faculty members is not intentional or the result of mean-spirited White and/or male faculty; rather it may be a matter of discomfort with the unfamiliar. Similarly, women and minority faculty will benefit from increased interaction with their senior colleagues. Sharing scholarship could be the common ground on which better relations and understanding are built.

Conclusion

There is much to be learned about the realities of women and minority faculty members. Individual institutions need to examine the climate for supporting a diverse faculty on their own campuses, and we also need more efforts to integrate these findings for broader understanding. As this review indicates, many parallels exist in the experiences of women and minority faculty across campuses; there are also likely to be parallels in what will work effectively to support these faculty. Colleges and universities can benefit from sharing both their problems and their responses.

The academic culture is challenged by a more diverse faculty. Traditional academic values of autonomy, competition, and individualism are called into question as women and, to some extent, minority faculty counter with values of community, connectedness, and collaboration. If colleges and universities genuinely seek to embrace a more diverse faculty, the academic culture will be affected. Adapting to change is never easy, but it would seem that there is much to be gained by rethinking the norms and traditions of the academy and reflecting upon how the scholarly community can best support a more diverse faculty. The three propositions offered here are intended not only to support women and minority faculty, but also to ultimately enhance the academic climate for the benefit of the entire academic community.

Note

1. In this review, the categories are reported exactly as they were used by the authors of the original sources. Every effort has been made to use comparable data sets.

References

Aisenberg, N., and Harrington, M. *Women of Academe: Outsiders in the Sacred Grove.* Amherst: University of Massachusetts Press, 1988.

Alpert, D. "Gender Inequity in Academia: An Empirical Analysis." *Initiatives,* 1989, 52, 9–14.

Armour, R., Fuhrmann, B., and Wergin, J. "Racial and Gender Differences in Faculty Careers." Paper presented at the American Educational Research Association, Boston, Apr. 1990.

Austin, A. E., and Pilat, M. "Tension, Stress, and the Tapestry of Faculty Lives." *Academe,* 1990, 76 (1), 38–42.

Banks, W. M. "Afro-American Scholars in the University: Roles and Conflicts." *American Behavioral Scientist,* 1984, 27, 325–339.

Boice, R. "Mentoring New Faculty: A Program for Implementation." *Journal of Staff, Program and Organizational Development,* 1990, 8, 143–160.

Boice, R. "New Faculty Involvement of Women and Minorities." *Research in Higher Education,* in press.

Bourguignon, E., Blanshan, S. A., Chiteji, L., MacLean, K. J., Meckling, S. J., Sagaria, M. A., Shuman, A. E., and Taris, M. T. *Junior Faculty Life at Ohio State: Insights on Gender and Race.* Columbus: Ohio State University Press, 1987.

Bowen, H. R., and Schuster, J. H. *American Professors.* Oxford, England: Oxford University Press, 1986.

Brown, S. V. *Increasing Minority Faculty: An Elusive Goal.* Princeton, N.J.: Educational Testing Service, 1988.

Carnegie Foundation for the Advancement of Teaching. "Women Faculty Excel as Campus Citizens." *Change,* 1990, 22 (5), 39–43.

Clark, S. M., and Corcoran, M. "Perspectives on the Professional Socialization of Women Faculty: A Case of Accumulative Disadvantage." *Journal of Higher Education,* 1986, 57, 20–43.

Cole, J. R. *Fair Science: Women in the Scientific Community.* New York: Free Press, 1979.

Corcoran, M., and Clark, S. M. "Professional Socialization and Contemporary Career Attitudes of Three Faculty Generations." *Research in Higher Education,* 1984, 20, 131–153.

Davis, D. E., and Astin, H. S. "Life Cycle, Career Pattern and Gender Stratification in Academe: Breaking Myths and Exposing Truths." In S. Lie and V. E. O'Leary (eds.), *Storming the Tower: Women in the Academic World.* London: Kogan & Page, 1990.

"Earned Degrees, 1989–90." *Chronicle of Higher Education,* May 13, 1992, p. A37.

Elmore, C. J., and Blackburn, R. T. "Black and White Faculty in White Research Universities." *Journal of Higher Education,* 1983, 53, 1–15.

Ervin, D., Thomas, B. J., and Zey-Ferrell, M. "Sex Discrimination and Rewards in a Public Comprehensive University." *Human Relations,* 1984, 37, 1005–1028.

Eveslage, S. A., Stonewater, B., and Dingerson, M. "Faculty Perceptions of Their Career Helping Relationships." Paper presented at the annual meeting of the Association for the Study of Higher Education, Baltimore, Nov. 1987.

Exum, W. H. "Climbing the Crystal Stair: Values, Affirmative Action, and Minority Faculty." *Social Problems,* 1983, 30 (4), 383–399.

Exum, W. H., Menges, R. J., Watkins, B., and Berglund, P. "Making It at the Top: Women and Minority Faculty in the Academic Labor Market." *American Behavioral Scientist,* 1984, 27, 301–324.

Farley, J. "Women Professors in the USA: Where Are They?" In S. Lie and V. E. O'Leary (eds.), *Storming the Tower: Women in the Academic World.* London: Kogan & Page, 1990.

Ferren, A. S. "Faculty Development Can Change the Culture of a College." *To Improve the Academy,* 1989, 8, 101–116.

Finkelstein, M. *The American Academic Profession: A Synthesis of Social Scientific Inquiry Since World War II.* Columbus: Ohio State University Press, 1984.

Hensel, N. *Realizing Gender Equality in Higher Education: The Need to Integrate Work/Family Issues.* ASHE-ERIC Higher Education Report No. 2. Washington, D.C.: School of Education and Human Development, George Washington University, 1991.

Johnsrud, L. K., and Atwater, C. D. *Barriers to Retention and Tenure at UH-Manoa: The Experiences of Faculty Cohorts 1982–1988.* Honolulu: Office of Academic Affairs, University of Hawaii at Manoa, 1991.

Johnsrud, L. K., and Atwater, C. D. "Barriers to the Retention and Tenure of Women and Minorities: The Case of a University's Faculty." Paper presented at the American Educational Research Association, San Francisco, Apr. 1992.

Justiz, M. J., Bjork, L. G., and Wilson, R. "Minority Faculty Opportunities in Higher Education." In M. J. Justiz and L. G. Bjork (eds.), *Higher Education Research and Public Policy.* New York: American Council on Education/Macmillan, 1988.

Kaufman, D. R. "Associational Ties in Academe: Some Male and Female Differences." *Sex Roles,* 1978, 4, 9–21.

Kritek, P. "Women's Work and Academic Sexism." *Educational Record*, 1984, *65*, 56–57.

Luz Reyes, M. L., and Halcon, J. J. "Racism in Academia: The Old Wolf Revisited." *Harvard Educational Review*, 1988, *58*, 229–314.

McElrath, K. "Gender, Career Disruption, and Academic Awards." *Journal of Higher Education*, 1992, *63*, 269–281.

McEvans, A. E., and Appelbaum, D. "Minority Faculty in Research Universities: Barriers to Progress." Paper presented at the American Educational Research Association, San Francisco, Apr. 1992.

Menges, R. J., and Exum, W. H. "Barriers to the Progress of Women and Minority Faculty." *Journal of Higher Education*, 1983, *54*, 123–143.

Montgomery, M. B. "The Decision to Have Children: Women Faculty in Social Work." *Affilia*, 1989, *4* (2), 73–84.

Moore, K. M., and Sagaria, M.A.D. "The Situation of Women in Research Universities in the United States: Within the Inner Circles of Academic Power." In G. P. Kelly and S. Slaughter (eds.), *Women's Higher Education in Comparative Perspective*. Dordrecht, Netherlands: Kluwer, 1991.

National Center for Education Statistics. *Digest of Education Statistics 1991*. Washington, D.C.: Office of Educational Research and Improvement, U.S. Department of Education, 1991.

O'Leary, V. E., and Mitchell, J. M. "Women Connecting with Women: Networks and Mentors." In S. Lie and V. E. O'Leary (eds.), *Storming the Tower: Women in the Academic World*. London: Kogan & Page, 1990.

Olsen, D., Maple, S. A., and Stage, F. "Women and Minority Faculty Job Satisfaction: A Structural Model Examining the Effect of Professional Role Interests, Professional Satisfactions, and Institutional Fit." Paper presented at the Association for the Study of Higher Education, Boston, Nov. 1991.

Parsons, L. A., Sands, R. G., and Duane, J. "The Campus Climate for Women Faculty at a Public University." *Initiatives*, 1991, *54*, 19–27.

Parsons, L. A., Sands, R. G., and Duane, J. "Sources of Career Support for University Faculty." *Research in Higher Education*, 1992, *33* (2), 161–176.

Persell, C. H. "Gender, Rewards and Research in Education." *Psychology of Women Quarterly*, 1983, *8*, 33–47.

Rausch, D. K., Ortiz, B. P., Douthitt, R. A., and Reed, L. L. "The Academic Revolving Door: Why Do Women Get Caught?" *CUPA Journal*, 1989, *40*, 1–16.

Reynolds, A. "Knowing One's World: Gender and World View in a Research University Culture." Paper presented at the American Educational Research Association, San Francisco, Mar. 1989.

Russell, S. H. "The Status of Women and Minorities in Higher Education: Findings from the 1988 National Survey of Postsecondary Findings." *CUPA Journal*, 1991, *42*, 1–11.

Smart, J. C. "Sex Equity in Academic Rank and Salary." *Review of Higher Education*, 1991, *14*, 511–526.

Smelser, N. J., and Content, R. *The Changing Academic Market*. Berkeley: University of California Press, 1980.

Sorcinelli, M. D., and Andrews, P. H. "Articulating Career Goals: A Comparison of Male and Female University Faculty." *Journal of NAWDAC*, 1987, *50*, 11–19.

Sorcinelli, M. D., and Near, J. P. "Relations Between Work and Life Away from Work Among University Faculty." *Journal of Higher Education*, 1989, *60* (1), 59–81.

Teevan, J. J., Pepper, S., and Pellizzari, J. R. "Academic Employment Decisions and Gender." *Research in Higher Education*, 1992, *33* (2), 141–159.

Touchton, J. G., and Davis, L. *Fact Book on Women in Higher Education*. New York: American Council on Education/Macmillan, 1991.

Turner, J. L., and Boice, R. "Experiences of New Faculty." *Journal of Staff, Program and Organizational Development*, 1989, *7*, 51–57.

U.S. Bureau of the Census. *Statistical Abstract of the U.S. 1991.* Washington, D.C.: U.S. Department of Commerce/U.S. Government Printing Office.

Whitt, E. " 'Hit the Ground Running': Experiences of New Faculty in a School of Education." *Review of Higher Education,* 1991, *14* (2), 177–197.

Wunsch, M. A., and Johnsrud, L. K. "Breaking Barriers: Mentoring Junior Faculty Women for Professional Development and Retention." *To Improve the Academy,* 1992, *11,* 175–187.

Yoder, J. D. "An Academic Woman as Token: A Case Study." *Journal of Social Issues,* 1985, *41,* 61–72.

LINDA K. JOHNSRUD is assistant professor in the Department of Educational Administration, University of Hawaii at Manoa.

From the early years of schooling through graduate training, women and minorities face institutional, social, and psychological factors that impede access and advancement.

Ivy Halls and Glass Walls: Barriers to Academic Careers for Women and Ethnic Minorities

Phyllis Bronstein, Esther D. Rothblum, Sondra E. Solomon

Academic departments seeking to increase the ethnic and cultural diversity of their faculty frequently come up empty-handed. Though search committees may follow all the appropriate affirmative action guidelines for locating and recruiting applicants from underrepresented groups, the ultimate applicant pool often turns out to be exclusively Caucasian. In regard to achieving gender balance, the picture is somewhat different. Over the past twenty years, increasing numbers of women have been hired for entry-level academic positions. While this appears to redress the gender imbalance that existed, the reality is that the overall proportion of women faculty has remained about the same, since the total number of faculty has itself increased over that time period (Blum, 1991; Johnsrud, this volume).

Further, that proportion is underrepresentative of the numbers of women who *could* be entering academia, if one looks at earlier career orientation. In the sciences in particular, slightly more women than men study science at the undergraduate level, but fewer women than men enroll in graduate-level science courses. By the time the doctorate is received, the numbers of women have shrunk dramatically; for example, in 1986 women received only 10 percent of the doctorates in chemistry and were appointed to only 4 percent of the entry-level academic positions (Hensel, 1989). Recent figures in neuroscience show that women represent 45 percent of entering graduate students, 38 percent of the Ph.D.'s awarded, and only 18 percent of the tenure-track jobholders (Barinaga, 1992). In addition, when women do enter academia, they tend to be hired at lower levels and at less-prestigious institutions than their male counterparts (American Association of University Women, 1989; Blum, 1991; Bronstein, Black, Pfennig, and White, 1986, 1987; Sandler and Hall, 1986).

If institutions of higher education are to achieve their stated goals of gender balance and multicultural diversity within their faculties, they must first learn to understand the factors that have impeded progress in that direction. This chapter will focus on the results of informal interviews with twelve women and members of ethnic minority groups who have made choices about entering academia, including graduate students, current faculty members, and individuals with graduate training who did not seek an academic career. (Details about individuals have been omitted, and in some instances modified, to protect their identity.) We will examine the institutional, social, and psychological factors at key points in time that may be serving as clearly visible barriers, or *invisible* ones—the glass walls—preventing women and people of color from making that career choice.

Institutional Factors

This section will examine early educational experiences as well as undergraduate and graduate experiences.

Early Educational Experiences. Most future academics seem to make their career choice during their undergraduate years. For women and people of color, however, paths that may lead to academia may not even be perceived, because of the messages embedded in the educational process from the time they enter school. Studies of classroom interaction and teacher attitudes from preschool through high school have found that teachers tend to show more attention to boys than to girls, and exert more effort to foster boys' cognitive development (American Association of University Women Educational Foundation, 1992; Sadker and Sadker, 1985; Serbin and O'Leary, 1979; Wilkenson and Marrett, 1985). In addition, teachers have been found to pay less attention to African American girls than to White girls (American Association of University Women Educational Foundation, 1992) and to give more negative academic and behavioral feedback to Black than to White children, and White teachers have been found to have more negative attitudes and beliefs about Black children than about White children (Irvine, 1985). It is not very surprising, then, that girls and ethnic minority children overall come to internalize these kinds of negative messages about their academic potential, and that these messages serve as barriers to making academic career choices. In fact, girls experience a loss in self-confidence in the early adolescent years that is twice that which boys experience (American Association of University Women, 1991). Some of our female (nonminority) respondents spoke of having been ignored or discounted by teachers, and the effects those messages had on them:

By my senior year in high school I had learned how to smile and gaze blankly at my male teachers, and never to volunteer anything in class.

I must have been very convincing, because when I scored very high in my county on a state scholarship exam, my [male] chemistry teacher said, "How did *you* ever manage to do that?"

When I went to my tenth high school reunion, I ran into my senior history teacher. I was surprised that he remembered me, since I had not been one of the special group of students (mainly male) he'd selected to meet with him after school, to discuss current events. He said to me, "You were always so smart—why didn't you ever say anything in class?" I remember thinking afterward, "Why didn't you ask me that ten years ago?"

Messages recalled by women of color were often more overt:

I was in the high honors group in high school, but was having trouble with freshman algebra. My teacher ignored me when I raised my hand or asked for extra help. However, I managed to pull my grade up to a B. When the teacher found out I wanted to go to college, she said she didn't think I was the kind of person who was acceptable for college, and flunked me for the year.

I was blackballed from being admitted to the National Honor Society my junior year in high school, by a teacher who said my behavior was a disgrace to my race, and I wouldn't be an asset to the Honor Society. My folks went to school and screamed bloody murder, so she couldn't do it again the next year, and I got in.

Ethnic minority men recalled similar negative messages:

When I was in first or second grade, there were two reading groups, the Bluebirds and the Redbirds. The Bluebirds were the good readers. I was in the Redbirds, though there had never been any test to determine reading ability. One day, I was asked to read aloud in class, and I read very well—and I was immediately put into the Bluebirds. I suddenly realized that I was the only Black kid in the Bluebirds, and that all of the Redbirds were Black.

My high school counselor never talked to me about college. When I said I was interested in going to college, he said that there were a lot of great trades opening up, and I might not want to waste my time with college.

In addition, studies of college entrance and scholarship exams have shown them to be very concrete barriers to academic advancement for women, ethnic minorities, and students from low-income families. Not only are they biased in item content, but they are biased in their predictions of academic performance. Specifically, average SAT scores are sixty-one points higher for males, yet females receive higher grades than males throughout both high school and college. In addition, as a result of lower test scores on the PSAT, girls receive only about one-third of the National Merit Scholarships, and lose out on many other scholarships from government and private agencies, who rely on PSAT, SAT, or ACT results to select winners ("Girls Lose Millions in Aid Because of Sex Bias," 1987; Rosser, 1987, 1989; "Tests Judged Unfair to Women," 1987). Ethnic minority girls face double jeopardy, since similar gaps between male and female scores exist within every ethnic group, and ethnic minorities overall score lower than Whites. This means that female and ethnic minority students will be less likely to gain admission to more-prestigious institutions, and, as a result of receiving fewer scholarships, will be more likely than White males to attend state and community colleges, rather than those private colleges and research universities that open the way to graduate school (see discussion below). The widespread tendency for students with financial means to obtain coaching for these exams further exacerbates the discrimination.

Undergraduate Environments. Those who go on to higher education are likely to continue to encounter subtle negative messages, which can create invisible walls. Trujillo (1986), in a study of the classroom behavior of White male professors toward minority and nonminority students at a large coeducational university, found that professors directed a greater number of complex questions to nonminority students, gave them more clues to help them improve their responses, and took more time in responding to questions those students posed. A study of classroom interaction in Harvard undergraduate classes (Krupnick, 1985) revealed that White male students tended to dominate discussion, particularly in classes with male teachers and a majority of male students, with White women and ethnic minority students of either gender playing a subordinate role. Further, in a study (Welch, cited in Krupnick, 1985) comparing classroom interaction at several Ivy League institutions, the women at coeducational schools were found to be much less assertive than those at all-female schools. Since most undergraduate institutions are coeducational and predominantly White, and most faculty are male, the classroom climates described in the first two examples above are more likely to represent the normative undergraduate experience, with White male students volunteering sooner and more frequently in class, speaking longer and with fewer interruptions, and male faculty encouraging this pattern (Krupnick, 1985).

Another factor that creates invisible walls is the interpersonal climate: whom students see, or do not see, on a daily basis in their institution. In research universities and prestigious four-year colleges, which are the institutions that are most likely to be grooming students for academic careers, there are very few faculty of color at any level, and relatively few tenured female faculty (Sandler and Hall, 1986; Johnsrud, this volume). Thus role models and mentors are rarely present for female and ethnic minority students: no one is encouraging and guiding them toward academic careers, and no one is showing them how it is done. Women undergraduates in the sciences and students of color in every area of predominantly White institutions are also likely to see few students like themselves, which may cause them to question whether they themselves belong there. One African American graduate student reported a common problem:

> I was the only Black student majoring in psychology in my college, and I felt very isolated. The other Black students kept asking me why I was wasting my time in that field, implying that it was a weird field for a Black to be in.

In addition, in this country, socioeconomic factors interact with culture, ethnicity, and gender in predicting academic and career attainment (American Association of University Women Educational Foundation, 1992; Arnold, 1993) and this interaction creates further barriers to academic careers for students of color. Specifically, because such students are more likely to have very limited financial resources, they are more likely to attend low-cost institutions, such as community and state colleges. Since these colleges emphasize teaching rather than faculty research, these students will then have little—if any—opportunity to develop interest or gain experience in research; furthermore, the faculty are likely to have less knowledge about helping students get into graduate school, and less tendency to steer their students in that direction. Thus, a sizeable number of ethnic minority undergraduates will never get on a graduate school "track." Even for those who are outstanding scholars in high school, family and cultural dictates may severely curtail educational and career attainment (Arnold, 1993). In addition, for those who are considering further education, degrees in business, law, or medicine are likely to seem a better return for all the money and time that will be invested in earning an advanced degree.

Graduate Education. For students who do wish to go on to graduate school, gender, race, and socioeconomic factors may again play a part in the process. While many graduate programs actively seek to admit members of underrepresented groups, invisible walls may affect the outcome. A White man and woman, respectively, both of whom did go on to become academics, offered interesting contrasting experiences:

> I decided on a career in sociology, and went to talk to the president [of a small, midwestern state college], to find out how to do that. He said, "Where do you want to go, Harvard, Princeton, or Yale?" On his advice, I applied to all three, and ended up at Yale.

In my early thirties, I became interested in psychology. I had a masters and a teaching job in another field, and I began taking courses, to get some background. When I asked one of my professors how I could go on in psychology, he told me that I would never get into graduate school because I had no math background and wouldn't be able to do the statistics, and besides, if I ever did get through graduate school, no one would hire me, because I would be too old. Luckily, I didn't listen. Two years later, I was coteaching the course with him.

Cultural differences, compounded with geographic and socioeconomic differences, may create invisible barriers for ethnic minority individuals applying to graduate school. They may be more likely to lack the financial resources for paying multiple application fees, visiting prospective institutions, and going on interviews—and they may have difficulty taking time away from employment to go through the application process. Faculty interviewers are more likely to respond favorably to the kind of social behaviors and self-presentation that are consonant with their own upbringing and education. The very small number of ethnic minority applicants may in itself create another invisible psychological barrier for those few who apply. One female graduate student spoke of her reactions when she took the Graduate Record Exam:

> There were very few Black or Hispanic faces in the room—and this was in New York City! I looked around and said to myself, "Where are we? Is everyone taking the GMAT's or the MCAT's or the LSAT's instead?" The question underneath that, of course, was, "When I get to graduate school, will I be the only one?"

Once they have entered graduate school, women and ethnic minority students are likely to find the same barriers they previously found, and new ones may appear. There is ample documentation that women are less likely to have mentors or to receive the same level of encouragement, resources, and opportunities as their male peers (American Association of University Women, 1989; Chamberlain, 1988; Gibbons, 1992; Sandler and Hall, 1986). The following reported experience is typical:

> My major professor never invited me to get involved in his research projects—he only worked with male students. The only mentoring he did was to say to me, in passing, "Maybe you should see about publishing those two group studies"—studies I had done, essentially on my own, four years previously. I wrote up and published the studies, with no additional input from him. And I never went to a conference, the whole time I was in graduate school—I never knew there were conferences.

Ethnic minority graduate students often have similar experiences. A Hispanic student reported that he and two other students of color (one African

American and one Asian American) had at different times asked a White faculty member if they could join his research team, only to be told that no new students were being added at that time. In each instance, the faculty member shortly thereafter added new White students to his team. Such incidents can cause women and ethnic minority students to question their own abilities, and their place in the academic world. In addition, students of color may suspect that both faculty and fellow students believe them to be less competent, and attribute their graduate school admission solely to affirmative action.

Because most graduate programs reflect the White, androcentric biases of the culture, it may be difficult for women and ethnic minority students to pursue scholarly interests that are especially meaningful for them. One group of feminist graduate students in psychology has written about the difficulty of pursuing feminist concerns in a department where "the mainstream perspective (that is, the White, middle-class, heterosexual, male perspective) . . . is taken as the status quo" (Six Spoke Collective, 1991, p. 104). An African American graduate student spoke of the lack of possibilities for collaborating on research related to African Americans, because there are no Black faculty or graduate students, aside from himself, in his department. In addition, the presence of women and ethnic minority faculty can have both positive and negative effects. On the one hand, they can serve as role models, offering support, guidance, and research opportunities for the students, with their presence attesting that there is a place for women and people of color in academia. On the other hand, such faculty much more frequently than their White male colleagues report that they feel unappreciated and unsupported in their departments, and that their work, particularly if it focuses on gender or minority issues, is devalued and viewed as peripheral (Bronstein, this volume; Rothblum, 1988). In addition, women and people of color are more likely to be denied reappointment or tenure, or to leave voluntarily within a few years of arriving (American Association of University Women, 1989; Blum, 1991; "Women Academics Still Experience Discrimination," 1986). Students who witness their role models being treated in this manner are likely to think twice before pursuing an academic career (Six Spoke Collective, 1991).

For the handful of ethnic minority graduate students who do decide to seek academic careers, the recent impetus to increase college and university faculty diversity has generally resulted in very positive outcomes to the job search process. For nonminority women, however, there may be additional barriers in the process, leading to less-than-optimal outcomes. Given the greater likelihood, compared with their male peers, that they have not been mentored, female graduate students are less likely to know how to make themselves marketable: how to publish their work, respond to reviewers, present at conferences, network with colleagues, prepare an effective curriculum vitae, or give a dynamic job talk. They are less likely to have someone pick up the phone on their behalf, to help them get a job via the Old Boys' network. If they have children, they are more likely to have male professors who will detail their family responsibilities in the letters of recommendation they write for them (Bronstein, Black, Pfennig, and White, 1986, 1987), thereby possibly prejudicing their applications. Departments considering their applications may tend to see them as less qualified than some of the men in the larger pool of male applicants, many of whom are recycling from tenure turn-downs and soft-money positions; such men often have longer publication records, simply because they have had a longer period of time since finishing graduate school to do research and publish their work. In addition, departments who already have one or two women often feel no imperative to hire more, even though the percentage of women faculty in the department is still far below the percentage in what affirmative action guidelines refer to as the availability pool (Bronstein, Black, Pfennig, and White, 1986, 1987). Thus, in many fields with predominantly male faculty, new female Ph.D.'s may still have difficulty getting tenure-track positions. Given the choice of spending several years in post-docs and visiting positions, in hopes of eventually landing a tenure-track appointment, some of these women look for careers outside of academia.

Social Factors

In addition to institutional factors, social factors also contribute to the glass walls keeping women and people of color from academic careers. These include family and relationship issues, life-style choices, and political climate.

In regard to family, the message to women that marriage and motherhood will be a key part of their adult identity begins in childhood, with the toys they are given (Langlois and Downs, 1980; Weinraub and Brown, 1983) and the doll play they see modeled in television commercials. Messages become more overt in adulthood, when families may pressure women to assume traditional roles. Two female faculty described these pressures:

> At a time when my career was going very well (I was doing a post-doc at Stanford), I went to a family wedding. The bride was unemployed, her brother was unemployed, and her sister had just broken up with her husband. But every single family member said to me, "I'm so sorry. I hope things get better soon." It took me a while to get what they were talking about—that I wasn't in a relationship!

> When I went on for my Ph.D., my mother seemed particularly uninterested and critical. Finally I said, "Aren't you proud of me?" And she said, "Of course I'm proud of you, but I disapprove of it six hundred percent!" She thought it was terrible that I didn't have any dining room furniture, and that I was neglecting my husband and children.

The message surfaces frequently in the media, often without any basis in fact. For example, *Newsweek* alarmed professional women across the country with a cover story on the purported odds against women in their thirties or older ever marrying (with 40-year-olds "more likely to be killed by a terrorist") (Salholz, 1986, p. 55). This widely-publicized claim was based on unpublished research which a population specialist at the Census Bureau was unable to replicate, but no correction or follow-up story was ever published (Faludi, 1991). A recent *New York Times Magazine* author bemoaned the shortage of educated African American men who could marry her daughter (Raybon, 1992). Instead of celebrating the increasing professional accomplishments of women, or examining the plight of African American males, the media has focused on the fact that some women might not get married, and presented this possibility as a cause for national concern.

Yet having both a family and an academic career is no simple matter. The tenure system in the United States was set up for male faculty, whose wives provided all the homemaking so that their husbands could devote their energies solely to academic career advancement. Such arrangements do not exist for most women faculty. It appears that the tendency for women to be concentrated in the lower faculty ranks and in non-tenure-track, part-time positions, is due in part to the conflicting demands of career and family relationships.

First, women who are married or in committed relationships more often than men put the needs of their partner ahead of their own career aspirations. They tend to be more hesitant to relocate, and more likely to limit their job seeking to locales where their partner can find suitable employment (Bronstein, Black, Pfennig, and White, 1986, 1987; Leviton and Whitely, 1981; Marwell, Rosenfeld, and Spilerman, 1979). Thus, for many female Ph.D.'s, living with one's partner means foregoing a tenure-track position (Barinaga, 1992)—or alternatively, obtaining a tenure-track position, and remaining single. Even before the job-seeking stage this gender difference is apparent: "My internship was for people going into academia, and all the interns (six women and seven men) came there from out of state. All the men were married, except one, and all of their wives came with them, and worked as secretaries and bank tellers—and that was what their work histories had been. All the women were single, except one, and the husband of the one who was married stayed in New Jersey." Further, women are more likely than men to view their relationship as an important priority, and to limit their working hours in order to maintain it, while men are likely to be less tolerant than women of their partner's devoting long hours to career demands.

Second, the decision to have children can present a major obstacle to academic advancement, or even to entering academia in the first place. If a woman has children before finishing graduate school, the demands of a tenure-track job, and the temporary relocations that may be required on the way to obtaining one, may seem too intimidating to contemplate. For those who do obtain tenure-track positions, the biological clock and the tenure clock are often ticking side by side, presenting women faculty with difficult decisions about whether to postpone either childbearing or tenure, or to drop off the tenure track altogether. Not surprisingly, promotions for women in academia take two to ten years longer than for men; women are less likely than men to be granted tenure (Hensel, 1989); and women are more likely than men to resign voluntarily from tenure-track positions (Rothblum, 1988). Overall, disproportionately fewer women achieve high levels of success in academia (Clark and Corcoran, 1986), with women reporting more conflict between parenting and work (Justus, Freitag, and Parker, 1987, cited in Hensel, 1989). Faculty women who have given birth during the pretenure period report that the demands of parenting made it difficult to find time to do research and writing (Hensel, 1989).

Women undergraduate and graduate students seem well aware of these dilemmas. One faculty member who attended an all-women's college said that her classmates always focused on the fact that very few of their female professors had both a career and a "normal" family life, and that fact caused them to steer away from an academic career. In fact, 50 percent of academic women remain single or childless (Hochschild, 1975); in a study of one university, no faculty women had had children before the age of thirty, compared with 75 percent of women in the population at large (Yogev and Vierra, 1983).

Potential life-style, philosophical, and political conflicts can also serve as social barriers to women considering entering academia. Women in our sample who chose to become psychotherapists rather than academics cited the desire to do "real-world" work, where they could retain their autonomy and "not be responsible to the patriarchy." Graduate students have noted such things as too little chance for collaborative work, too much focus on counting publications rather than the quality of the work, too little opportunity to effect social change, and the absence of role models who have shown that it is possible to work productively in academia and have leisure time (see Six Spoke Collective, 1991). Political obstacles that these women mentioned included concerns about how their feminism would be received, and whether it would impede their career advancement. Lesbians and gay men may have similar concerns regarding their sexual orientation, if they wish to be open about it to students, or if they wish to do research in this area (Rothblum, 1992; Tierney and Rhoads, this volume). For people of color, there may also be geographic barriers—jobs in certain parts of the country that seem impossible to consider, because of an absence of others from similar backgrounds, or because of the overall racial climate—including actual physical risks likely to be incurred by living in a racially hostile environment. Also, the five years it takes to go through graduate school, plus the additional seven to ten years it will take to earn tenure, can seem an inordinately long period for career building, especially for students from low-income or nonprofessional backgrounds.

Psychological Factors

Because people seem to internalize many of the messages they receive from the world around them, it is difficult to separate out psychological factors from institutional and social ones. Perhaps the psychological barriers to academia for women and people of color can be seen as end products: an internalization of the institutional and social oppression that causes the individual to become *self*-denigrating and *self*-limiting in thoughts and behaviors. These negative self-messages can take different forms. For women, there is frequently a sense of inadequacy around numbers and computers, which seems to be an outgrowth of the math anxiety that girls often "catch" beginning in fifth grade (Tobias, 1978). Each year some of our brightest female graduate students enlist male peers to do the data analyses on their projects—whereas we have yet to see a male graduate student seek that kind of assistance. Students with this sense of inadequacy will, of course, be less likely to make a career choice for which research is the key to success.

Writing is another major area of concern. Women and ethnic minority faculty frequently mention writing blocks, procrastination, and a sense of paralysis. For some, there is the fear that their writing will reveal inadequacies they suspect about themselves: lower intelligence, weak ideas, or even mistakes in grammar or vocabulary. Socioeconomic background can play an important part in these concerns, in terms of the ways that reading and writing were regarded in their families of origin, and the quality of the schools they attended. For others, it is more a question of voice. If they dare to write about what is meaningful to them, will it be regarded as too radical or tangential, and thus impede their career advancement (Bronstein, this volume; Six Spoke Collective, 1991)? Will they be dismissed, attacked, or thought crazy? Overall, it may also be a question of identity, that is, of seeing scholarship as their rightful calling (see Gainen, this volume). Because of all the messages to the contrary that women and people of color have encountered, in the educational system and the world at large, very few are able to respond as the late feminist scholar Nancy Datan (1982, p. 6) did, when her husband complained that she never cooked: "I write. I write books and I write essays and I write poetry. That's what I do."

The result of internalizing negative messages may be an overriding fear of failure. One woman faculty told us, "What many [women] students tell me is the reason for not going into academia is, 'I couldn't take the "publish or perish."' What I think this really means isn't job security, it's the tremendous evaluation anxiety—terror of what it would mean to be so publicly failing." Such fears contribute further to the writing difficulties described above. Research on procrastination in college students found that key factors for women, more than for men, were evaluation anxiety, perfectionism, and low self-esteem (Rothblum, Solomon, and Murakami, 1986; Solomon and Rothblum, 1984). These kinds of fears are at the basis of what Clance (1985) has described as the "imposter phenomenon," a sense of intellectual "faking" often experienced by high-achieving women. Since these feelings are likely to intensify the higher up the educational ladder they go, it is not surprising that many women and people of color choose not to enter academia, where performance evaluation occurs for every paper and grant proposal they submit, and every class they teach.

Conclusion

Given the visible and invisible barriers to academic careers that women and people of color currently encounter, what reasons might there be for them to pursue that goal? Clearly, academia is a route to social and political power; it brings automatic prestige, access to the media, access to political structures, and access to the promising young minds who will shape society's future. Thus, for individuals trying to address social, political, and economic inequities, an academic career can provide the means. Further, if we want women and ethnic minority students to feel welcome and less isolated in our academic programs, then there have to be mentors and role models to guide them. One faculty woman spoke of the choice she had made: "My daughters, having seen what a struggle it's been, and how much I work, have asked me if I would choose to do it again. And I've said yes. I'm really doing it for them—and for women—pushing the doors open a little wider, and holding them open. Some of us have to do that, and I've chosen to be one of the ones who tries to take that on." Finally, the talents and diverse perspectives that they bring can only serve to enrich the fields that they enter, and the rewards will be felt on every level—by individuals, disciplines, and institutions.

Recommendations. What, then, can be done to help women and people of color break through the glass walls blocking their entry into academic careers? Since socioeconomic level is such a strong predictor of academic achievement, it is possible to conclude that nothing will change until there is a more equitable distribution of resources in this country. However, we believe it is possible to make the glass walls visible, and to remove them.

During the primary and secondary school years school personnel can have an enormous impact. If teachers, guidance counselors, and administrators are to prevent and remove the barriers described here, they must become educated about sociocultural and gender inequities, and how they are played out within the school world. This education process should be part of both their undergraduate and graduate training. In addition, schools can help ethnic minority parents and parents of girls become more aware of these issues, so that they can most effectively foster their children's academic potential. Both schools and parents must also insist on financial parity for all students, so that there are equal academic and extracurricular resources available for girls and boys, and for all children of color. The use of college entrance examinations to keep the gates open wider for White males than for other groups must be challenged.

Much can be done in higher education as well. Colleges and universities must continue actively to recruit underrepresented groups into their student bodies. They must educate their faculty about the subtle ways that sexism and racism can limit academic advancement, and monitor teaching and advising with this in mind (see the guide published by the Association of American Colleges, 1992). They must provide incentives to administrators and faculty for retaining women and ethnic minority students, and fostering their academic advancement. They must provide mentors and role models, by hiring more women and people of color as faculty and upper-level administrators. And they must make their curricula gender-balanced and multicultural—for example, by establishing women's studies and various ethnic studies programs, by providing course offerings that focus on issues related to women and people of color, and by incorporating gender-related and multicultural material into existing courses. Colleges and universities must recruit aggressively at all levels, so that women and ethnic minorities are included in upper- as well as entry-level ranks, and so that the numbers within departments move beyond token representation. There must also be aggressive efforts at retention and promotion. This means standardizing and monitoring reappointment, tenure, and promotion procedures, so that they cannot be used as instruments of discrimination. It means creating a climate of support and respect for women and ethnic minority faculty—for example, by providing mentoring and equal resources, and showing interest in their work. It means building flexibility into appointments and tenure timetables, so that faculty women do not have to choose between academia and motherhood. It means attending to the issue of inclusion, in terms of appointments to key committees and decision-making bodies, and partici-pation in department social activities. Many resources are available that provide detailed guidelines for change within our institutions of higher education—in particular, publications from the Project on the Status and Education of Women of the Association of American Colleges, and the American Association of University Women. We now have the opportunity to reexamine our beliefs and practices, and to reeducate ourselves, so that we can remove the glass walls, and welcome many more women and people of color into careers in academia.

References

American Association of University Women. *Women and Tenure: The Opportunity of a Century.* Washington, D.C.: American Association of University Women, 1989.

American Association of University Women. *Shortchanging Girls, Shortchanging America.* Washington, D.C.: American Association of University Women, 1991.

American Association of University Women Educational Foundation. *The AAUW Report: How Schools Shortchange Girls.* Washington, D.C.: American Association of University Women, 1992.

Arnold, K. D. "The Fulfillment of Promise in African-American and Mexican-American High School Valedictorians and Salutatorians." *Review of Higher Education,* in press.

Association of American Colleges. *Teaching Faculty Members to Be Better Teachers: A Guide to Equitable and Effective Classroom Technique.* Washington, D.C.: Association of American Colleges, 1992.

Barinaga, M. "Profile of a Field: Neuroscience. The Pipeline Is Leaking." *Science,* 1992, *255,* 1366–1367.

Blum, D. E. "Environment Still Hostile to Women in Academe, New Evidence Indicates." *Chronicle of Higher Education,* Oct. 9, 1991, pp. A1, A20.

Bronstein, P., Black, L., Pfennig, J., and White, A. "Getting Academic Jobs: Are Women Equally Qualified—And Equally Successful?" *American Psychologist,* Mar. 1986, pp. 318–322.

Bronstein, P., Black, L., Pfennig, J., and White, A. "Stepping Onto the Academic Career Ladder: How Are Women Doing?" In B. A. Gutek and L. Larwood (eds.), *Women's Career Development.* Newbury Park, Calif.: Sage, 1987.

Chamberlain, M. K. *Women in Academe: Progress and Prospects.* New York: Russell Sage Foundation, 1988.

Clance, P. R. *The Imposter Phenomenon: When Success Makes You Feel Like a Fake.* New York: Bantam Books, 1985.

Clark, S., and Corcoran, M. "Perspectives on the Professional Socialization of Women Faculty: A Case of Accumulative Disadvantage?" *Journal of Higher Education,* 1986, *57* (1), 20–43.

Datan, N. "The Fifty-Nine Cent Cycle." Unpublished manuscript, West Virginia University, 1982.

Faludi, S. *Backlash: The Undeclared War on American Women.* New York: Crown, 1991.

Gibbons, A. "Key Issue: Two-Career Science Marriage." *Science,* 1992, *255,* 1380–1381.

"Girls Lose Millions in Aid Because of Sex Bias." *National NOW Times,* May–June 1987, p. 3.

Hensel, N. "Resolving the Conflict: Parenting and Professorship." *Thought and Action,* 1989, *5* (2), 71–84.

Hochschild, A. R. "Inside the Clockwork of Male Careers." In F. Howe (ed.), *Women and the Power to Change.* New York: McGraw-Hill, 1975.

Irvine, J. J. "Teacher Communication Patterns as Related to the Race and Sex of the Student." *Journal of Educational Research,* 1985, *78* (6), 338–345.

Justus, J., Freitag, S. B., and Parker, L. L. *The University of California in the Twenty-First Century: Successful Approaches to Faculty Diversity.* University of California, Berkeley, 1987.

Krupnick, C. G. "Women and Men in the Classroom: Inequality and Its Remedies." *Teaching and Learning,* 1985, *1* (1), 18–25.

Langlois, J. H., and Downs, A. C. "Mothers, Fathers, and Peers as Socialization Agents of Sex-Typed Play Behaviors in Young Children." *Child Development,* 1980, *51,* 1217–1247.

Leviton, L. C., and Whitely, S. E. "Job Seeking Patterns of Female and Male Ph.D. Recipients." *Psychology of Women Quarterly,* 1981, *5* (5), 690–701.

Marwell, G., Rosenfeld, R., and Spilerman, S. "Geographic Constraints on Women's Careers in Academia." *Science,* 1979, *205,* 1225–1231.

Raybon, P. "The Stolen Promise." *New York Times Magazine,* May 3, 1992, pp. 20–22.

Rosser, P. *Sex Bias in College Admissions Tests: Why Women Lose Out.* Cambridge, Mass.: National Center for Fair and Open Testing (FairTest), 1987.

Rosser, P. *The SAT Gender Gap: Identifying the Causes.* Washington, D.C.: Center for Women Policy Studies, 1989.

Rothblum, E. D. "Leaving the Ivory Tower: Factors Contributing to Women's Voluntary Resignation from Academia." *Frontiers,* 1988, *10* (2), 14–17.

Rothblum, E. D. "Issues Facing Lesbian and Gay Psychologists in Academic Settings." Unpublished manuscript, 1992.

Rothblum, E. D., Solomon, L. J., and Murakami, J. "Affective, Cognitive, and Behavioral Differences Between High and Low Procrastinators." *Journal of Counseling Psychology,* 1986, *33,* 387–394.

Sadker, M., and Sadker, D. "Sexism in the Schoolroom of the 80's." *Psychology Today,* Mar. 1985, pp. 54–57.

Salholz, E. "The Marriage Crunch." *Newsweek,* June 2, 1986, pp. 54–57, 61.

Sandler, B. R., and Hall, R. M. *The Campus Climate Revisited: Chilly for Women Faculty, Administrators, and Graduate Students.* Washington, D.C.: Project on the Status and Education of Women, Association of American Colleges, Oct. 1986.

Serbin, L. A., and O'Leary, D. K. "How Nursery Schools Teach Girls to Shut Up." In J. H. Williams (ed.), *Psychology of Women: Selected Readings.* New York: Norton, 1979.

Six Spoke Collective. "Feminism and Psychology: A Dangerous Liaison." *Women and Therapy,* 1991, *11* (1), 103–110.

Solomon, L. J., and Rothblum, E. D. "Academic Procrastination: Frequency and Cognitive-Behavioral Correlates." *Journal of Counseling Psychology,* 1984, *31,* 503–509.

"Tests Judged Unfair to Women." *Project on the Status and Education of Women,* 1987, *17* (2), 2–3.

Tobias, S. *Overcoming Math Anxiety.* New York: Norton, 1978.

Trujillo, C. M. "A Comparative Examination of Classroom Interaction Between Professors and Minority and Non-Minority College Students." *American Educational Research Journal,* 1986, *23* (4), 629–642.

Weinraub, M., and Brown, L. M. "The Development of Sex-Role Stereotypes in Children: Crushing Realities." In V. Franks and E. D. Rothblum (eds.), *The Stereotyping of Women: Its Effects on Mental Health.* New York: Springer, 1983.

Welch, K. "Sex Differences in Language and the Importance of Context: An Observational Study of Classroom Speech." Unpublished undergraduate thesis, Yale University, 1984.

Wilkinson, L. C., and Marrett, C. B. *Gender Influences in Classroom Interaction.* Orlando, Fla.: Academic Press, 1985.

"Women Academics Still Experience Discrimination." In *Higher Education and National Affairs.* Washington, D.C.: American Council on Education, 1986.

Yogev, S., and Vierra, A. "The State of Motherhood Among Professional Women." *Sex Roles,* 1983, *9,* 391–396.

PHYLLIS BRONSTEIN is associate professor of clinical psychology at the University of Vermont. She has done research on women's professional advancement in psychology, and is editor of Teaching the Psychology of People: Resources for Gender and Sociocultural Awareness.

ESTHER D. ROTHBLUM is associate professor of clinical psychology at the University of Vermont. She is editor of the journal Women and Therapy *and of the book* Treating Women's Fear of Failure.

SONDRA E. SOLOMON is a doctoral student in clinical psychology at the University of Vermont. Her research is on women and disability, and her dissertation is a study of ethnic minority women and physical distinction.

"Barrioization" and devaluation of Chicano/Latino faculty scholarship and community service maintain patterns of underrepresentation, which are compounded by the academy's unwillingness to scrutinize its own discriminatory practices.

Second-Class Academics: Chicano/Latino Faculty in U.S. Universities

Hisauro Garza

The Problem

Representation of Chicanos/Latinos in the U.S. professoriate remains the absolute lowest of all racial and ethnic groups when their proportion of the U.S. population is considered. As Figure 3.1 shows, in 1983 Chicanos/Latinos held only one third of the faculty posts they would have held if their numbers were proportional to the Chicano/Latino population at large, and this proportion appears to have declined between 1983 and 1989.[1] The bleak situation of Chicanos/Latinos regarding the attainment of doctorates over the last fifteen or twenty years (see Figure 3.2) means that the pool of eligible candidates for faculty positions remains small. Additionally, preliminary results of the 1990 U.S. Census show continued dramatic population growth for Chicanos/Latinos. Given this demographic situation, it is quite likely that the representation of Chicanos/Latinos in higher education has worsened.

Chicanos/Latinos remain conspicuously underrepresented at four-year universities, particularly the more prestigious ones. Indeed, just as Chicanos/Latinos are "better" represented in the lower ranks of the professoriate, lecturers and other junior faculty, and significantly less well represented in the higher ranks, such as associate and full professor, they are much "better" represented in two-year colleges than four-year institutions (García, 1980; Olivas, 1979). In California, for example, 5.1 percent of the community college faculty in 1981 was Hispanic, but only 2.5 percent of the California State University (CSU) system and 2.4 percent of the University of California system faculties were Hispanic (California Postsecondary Education Commission data supplied to me by the Office of the President, University

Figure 3.1. Full-Time Professors (All Ranks)

'83 adjusted for '80 Pop., '89 for '90

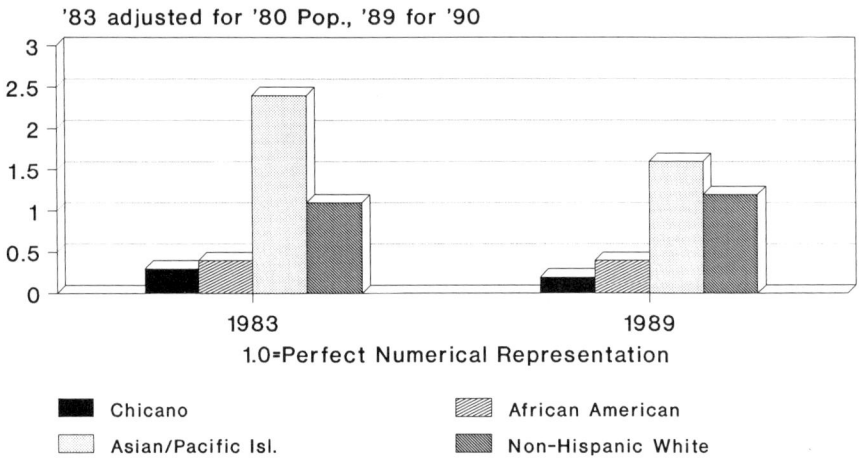

1.0=Perfect Numerical Representation

- Chicano
- Asian/Pacific Isl.
- African American
- Non-Hispanic White

Note: Figures for 1983 have been adjusted from 1980 population data, and those for 1989 have been adjusted from 1990 data.

Sources: Adapted from U.S. Equal Employment Opportunity Commission, 1983, 1989; U.S. Department of Commerce, 1980, 1990.

Figure 3.2. Annual Doctorates in the United States

'75 adjusted for '80 Pop., '89 for '90

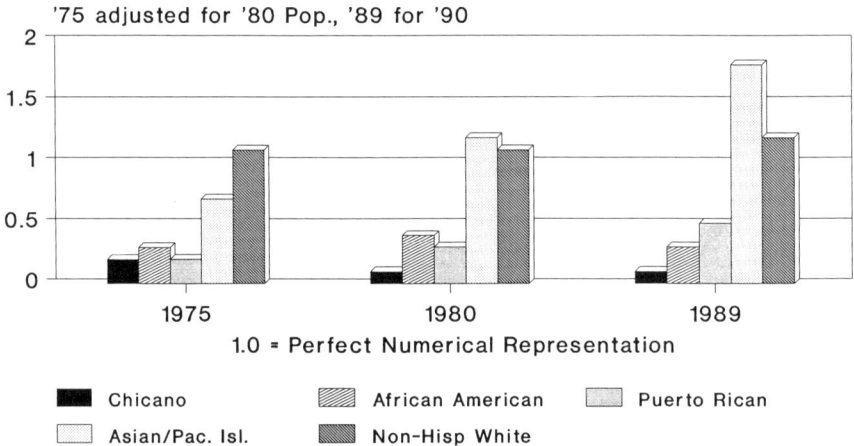

1.0 = Perfect Numerical Representation

- Chicano
- Asian/Pac. Isl.
- African American
- Non-Hisp White
- Puerto Rican

Note: Figures for 1975 have been adjusted from 1980 population data, and those for 1989 from 1990 data.

Sources: Adapted from U.S. Department of Commerce, 1980, 1990; National Research Council, 1975, 1980, 1989.

of California, Berkeley, April 14, 1986). Even California State University at Fresno, part of the CSU system that produces the largest percentage of all bachelors degrees in the United States awarded to Hispanics, was still quite below parity in the fall of 1988 in its percentage of Chicano/Latino faculty, given regional and state population proportions. While Chicano/Latino students made up 16.9 percent of the total student body, their counterparts among the faculty totalled a mere 5.0 percent (Chicano/Latino Faculty Association, personal communication, 1989).

Moreover, in times of economic crisis, Chicano/Latino and other newly hired minority faculty may be the most at risk. For example, even as I wrote this article in mid 1992, the California state government was facing one of its worst fiscal crises in the last fifty years. Heavy cutbacks have already hit the educational system, including the California State University system. Over the last two or three weeks scores of professors received layoff notices. The California Faculty Association, the official collective bargaining unit for the CSU faculty, has so far pushed for the *seniority* system as the main criterion for determining which faculty members will be laid off and which will be retained. Little discussion is taking place on the inevitable disastrous effects on Chicano/Latino and other racial and ethnic minority faculty of the use of this single criterion. By my rough calculations, as many as 40 to 60 percent of the total Chicano/Latino faculty could be laid off, reversing any gains that have been made in recent years. When existing tenure status, professorial rank, and seniority systems are invoked to trim back faculties and programs, especially in the current period of fiscal austerity, relative newcomers to academe overwhelmingly carry the brunt of tenure denials and layoffs (Boulding, 1983; Elmore and Blackburn, 1983; Vander Waerdt, 1982).

The numbers of minority professors are seriously threatened by several factors: (1) the stabilization at a low level or a decrease in the numbers of undergraduate and graduate enrollments for Chicanos/Latinos; (2) the more pragmatic nature of graduate majors due to the sagging national economy of the last ten or twelve years; and (3) the likelihood that depressed faculty salaries, restricted faculty employment opportunities, and general loss of status of professors over the last decade may have made college teaching significantly less appealing to young people. Moreover, messages concerning the negative evaluation of minority scholars and their scholarship within academia must certainly get out to potential candidates and act as a damper on the number of those who are considering whether to pursue doctoral studies and later apply for faculty positions. A significant decline in the already low number of minority professors, particularly as a percentage of total faculty, is the most probable scenario for at least the remainder of the 1990s.

The evidence just presented suggests that affirmative action has failed. The pattern of underrepresentation of minorities within the U.S. professorate continues with little or no sign of major improvement in the future. In the 1984 Carnegie Faculty Survey only 56.1 percent of the faculty surveyed believed that affirmative action had increased the number of minority group members on their faculty ("New Carnegie Data Show Faculty Members Uneasy," 1985). In my own 1987 national survey of Chicano/Latino faculty, described below, this opinion about the failure of affirmative action is even more pronounced. Seventy-four percent of Chicano/Latino faculty stated that they do not believe affirmative action is working effectively to bring members of their own groups to their universities.

In their large-scale study of the American professoriate, *American Professors: A National Resource Imperiled,* Bowen and Schuster (1986, p. 152) note that "no aspect of our campus visits was more alarming than the situation we found with respect to minority faculty members. Over the past two decades, higher education has made considerable progress in opening the faculty to ethnic minorities, but that movement seems to have ground to a halt and may even be in reverse gear. Almost everywhere we went, we were struck by the scarcity of minority faculty." The failure of affirmative action can be traced in part to a system of university-entrenched values and racism that negatively impacts racial/ethnic minorities. As the dean of the faculty at Amherst College stated in the *New York Times,* "In my contacts with a considerable range of academic institutions, I have become aware of pervasive residues of racism and sexism, even among those whose intentions and conscious beliefs are entirely nondiscriminatory" (quoted in Schwartz, 1984, p. 61). To begin to reverse these patterns, we must understand the role and status of Chicano/Latino faculty members and their experiences of academic life.

"*Barrioization*" of Chicano/Latino Faculty

Associated with the issue of representation in academia are the issues of the location and treatment of those Chicanos/Latinos who do make it into universities as faculty members. Recent research shows that these faculty are often concentrated heavily in Chicano/Latino studies, ethnic studies, or departments such as Spanish language and literature or bilingual education. They tend to participate in university committees of limited scope such as those dealing with cultural matters, study abroad, and student recruitment. In this way, universities create and maintain affirmative action "dumping grounds," university enclaves with little connection to the university's mainstream curriculum and scholarly life. This racially and ethnically insidious "ghettoization" or, since it involves Chicanos/Latinos, "*barrioization*" (Garza, 1988), contributes to the formation of "separate but equal" racial/ethnic divisions that fuel the misperception of Chicano/Latino scholarship as political partisanship and advocacy rather than true, legitimate research and scholarship in its own right. Besides being concentrated, compartmentalized, and isolated in a few departments, Chicano/Latino faculty believe that they are viewed as second-class academics because they and their teaching, research, and publications are undervalued.

Furthermore and paradoxically, the limited presence of Chicanos/Latinos as university faculty may itself reinforce the perception that they do not belong in the university since they tend to be seen as "affirmative action hires." This further contributes to their unacceptability and illegitimacy as scholars. In his article "The Protection of the Inept" Goode (1967, p. 5) observes that "the privileged . . . try systematically to prevent the talent of the less privileged from being recognized or developed." Karen (1990, p. 235) more recently remarks that "dominant groups are able to establish the specific cultural content that defines what it means to be meritorious." These are important ways in which social systems maintain the status quo of social inequalities in society generally, and in academia particularly.

Faculty Perceptions and Experiences

In order to describe the treatment and status of Chicano/Latino professors, I will use data from the National Latino Faculty Survey (NLF Survey) of Chicano/Latino faculty at four-year colleges and universities (Garza, 1987). A twenty-three-page questionnaire was mailed to 519 randomly selected Chicano/Latino faculty. An adjusted questionnaire return rate of 62 percent was obtained (N = 238). Faculty were selected if they (1) had a Spanish surname; (2) taught in humanities, social sciences, education, or ethnic studies departments; and (3) were employed by four-year institutions in the continental United States. Data were analyzed to compare faculty who had been denied tenure with those who had not (either currently tenured or not yet tenured).

The survey indicated that Chicano/Latino professors subscribe to traditional scholarly and academic values at a very high rate. For example, nine out of ten Chicano/Latino faculty respondents consider themselves "intellectuals" (90 percent) and "scholars" (93 percent). Nearly nine out of ten (85 percent) are "committed to the rules and standards for scientific pursuits." However, while the overwhelming majority of them subscribe to traditional academic values, many do not feel "their" colleges or universities believe in them. They tend to feel that they are not truly accepted as equals, as scholars in their own right by the same university community that promotes these scientific ideals.

For example, a surprisingly large number (44 percent) of Chicano and Puerto Rican professors feel that research *by* Chicanos and Puerto Ricans is seen as academically inferior and illegitimate in their own departments. This perception was even more widespread among faculty at the more prestigious universities. Additionally, two out of every five Chicanos and Puerto Ricans feel that their departmental colleagues also devalue research *on* the subject of their own racial/ethnic group. Nine out of ten feel that academic research on their own group is rated as being of low quality (45 percent), or rated higher (40 percent) when this kind of research is carried out by non-Latino Whites. These scholars feel that negative evaluation by their departments is directed at both their topics of research and themselves as researchers. This scholarly dilemma is perhaps best exemplified by the comments of a Puerto Rican professor specializing in economic development of the Caribbean and Latin America: "There seems to be the assumption that all Latinos teach or should teach ethnic studies. . . . The problem is not that Anglos consider ethnic studies inferior, but Latinos in general inferior whether they do ethnic studies or not."

Tenure

This broad negative valuation reflects the most crucial of all academic rites of passage: the award of tenure. For example, among the twenty-one Chicano/Latinos in the NLF Survey who reported being denied tenure, the top three reasons named for being denied tenure were "departmental politics" and "discrimination/racism" (both tied for the highest reason), and "insensitivity to their research interests and perspectives" (second highest reason). Members of the group that was denied tenure were identical in most respects, including publication of articles and books, to members of the group not denied tenure. The main difference between these two groups is that those denied tenure were more likely to: (1) be involved in research, teaching, and publishing on the subject of their "own ethnic and/or Latino/ Hispanic groups"; (2) feel that research on and by Latinos is seen as "academically inferior and illegitimate"; and (3) feel that faculty in their departments are "not very qualified" or "unqualified" to evaluate their research. They are also more likely to feel a sense of not belonging in their departments and not being accepted as scholarly equals.

When the work of racial/ethnic minority scholars is devalued, the struggle for tenure becomes more problematic. NLF Survey data show that one in three Chicano/Latino faculty members (34 percent) surveyed felt that it either was or would be more difficult for them to receive tenure compared to Anglos or other non-Chicanos/Latinos in their respective departments. In a 1978 survey of 321 graduate chairpersons of psychology departments, Stapp found that tenure rates of minorities were comparable to those for nonminority men. However, she also found significantly greater numbers of minorities, particularly minority men, leaving their faculty appointments before receiving tenure. "That is," states Stapp, "they are caught in a 'revolving door'; minorities and women are brought in, then they are passed over for promotion [or tenure] and they are back out the door again" (1979, p. 14). In that study, 36.9 percent of minority men, compared to only 18.9 percent of nonminority men, left the department before the tenure decision was made.

Compounding the difficulties of negative valuation are the many pressures and demands on their time experienced by Chicano/Latino faculty. Among the top reasons (ranked fifth out of eighteen reasons) psychology department chairpersons state for the lack of tenure among minorities is "Being given too heavy teaching/advising/committee load" (Suinn and Witt, 1982). Chicano/Latino professors often seem to have heavier teaching loads and responsibilities, in part because they are concentrated in colleges and universities where their workloads are significantly heavier (California Faculty Association, 1990; Suinn and Witt, 1982).

Since quite often a Chicano/Latino may be the only Chicano/Latino in the department, he or she is highly sought after to participate in a plethora of minority-related committee meetings. Moreover, because of his or her singular status, nearby Latino communities and fellow-ethnic university students also make multiple demands on his or her time. In the NLF Survey, three out of four Chicano and Puerto Rican faculty expressed the belief that they have greater demands made on their time than do Anglo or other non-Chicano/Latino professors. These demands often come from active political communities within the larger Chicano/Latino community.

However, these forms of "minority service" do not enhance the Chicano/Latino scholar's application for tenure and promotion. In spite of genuine contributions by these scholars in local communities, "minority service," as Suinn and Witt (1982) note, if used at all as a basis for tenure, is negatively evaluated. "Too much minority service" was seen by psychology department chairpersons as the number-one obstacle to minorities' receiving tenure. Involvement in "too much minority service" seems to have a negative impact on minority faculty in at least two important ways: (1) in directly distracting the minority scholar from research, writing, and publishing; and (2) in engaging in an activity that is itself negatively evaluated and/or is seen by others as impeding "true scholarship" by these newcomer academics.

Directions for Change

Significant changes need to be carried out within universities in their treatment and evaluation of minorities and their scholarship. The changes that began to take place in society at large as the result of progressive social legislation passed in the 1960s, although often aided by research emanating from universities, seems to have had only a limited counterpart in the world of the academy itself. While U.S. scholars surveyed, measured, and analyzed the social inequalities in the rest of their society, they largely ignored their own backyard. They did not study themselves and the barriers to equality in the university itself. Academics need to reassess what constitutes rigorous and legitimate scholarship, and its relationship to institutional barriers that may help maintain ethnic and racial social divisions. Most of the national and international politics and principal movements for change of at least the last quarter century centered on racial and ethnic group matters. Therefore, this kind of scholarship and the scholars who do it should be accorded the necessary respect and legitimacy it and they deserve.

The need for professors and researchers from within the Chicano/Latino group, and particularly Chicanos and Puerto Ricans, is great. It is these individuals who often focus attention on important social issues. Their research spans educational and economic opportunity issues, immigration, health, community studies, voting patterns, and the intersection of class, race, and gender in issues of social inequality. They play key roles as researchers, lecturers, advisers and spokespersons, often (although not always) addressing issues about Chicanos/Latinos and other racial/ethnic minorities.

Besides contributing generally through their roles as researchers and teachers to the advancement of learning and culture, they also contribute directly to the personal development of the young minds and leaders of each generation. Their presence on campus makes the expectations and experience of undergraduate and graduate students that much more meaningful and credible, since many of these scholars have struggled to attain their own education and career. This puts them in particularly strategic positions as role models to provide the necessary and important mentoring, motivation, and social sponsorship necessary for Chicano/Latino students to enroll, stay, and succeed in college and to continue through graduate education. They help create a culturally diverse, relevant, receptive, and supportive university setting. They enrich the university context, while making it relevant and responsive to the needs of previously ignored Americans. These issues become increasingly pressing as the number of Chicanos/Latinos continues to grow, putting them rapidly on their way to becoming the largest combined racial and ethnic group in the United States.

Note

1. The proportions given in Figures 3.1 and 3.2 were derived by dividing the percentages that each racial/ethnic group makes up of the total U.S. doctorates awarded (Figure 3.1) and of the total full-time faculty (Figure 3.2) by the percentage that each of these groups made up in the U.S. population for each of the two decennial census years (1980 and 1990).

References

Boulding, E. "Minorities and Women: Even Harder Times." *Academe,* 1983, 69 (1), 27–28.
Bowen, H. R., and Schuster, J. H. *American Professors: A National Resource Imperiled.* New York: Oxford University Press, 1986.

California Faculty Association. *CSU Faculty Workload Study.* Fullerton: California State University, 1990.

Elmore, C. J., and Blackburn, R. T. "Black and White Faculty in White Research Universities." *Journal of Higher Education,* 1983, *54* (1), 1–15.

García, R. "The Contradiction of Access: A Study of Chicano Participation in Colleges and Universities of the Southwest." Unpublished doctoral dissertation, University of Michigan, 1980.

Garza, H. "National Latino Faculty Survey." Unpublished data, University of California, Berkeley, 1987.

Garza, H. "The 'Barrioization' of Hispanic Faculty." *Educational Record,* 1988, *69* (1), 122–124.

Goode, W. J. "The Protection of the Inept." *American Sociological Review,* 1967, *32.*

Karen, D. "Toward a Political-Organizational Model of Gatekeeping: The Case of Elite Colleges." *Sociology of Education,* 1990, *63,* 227–240.

National Research Council. Office of Scientific and Engineering Personnel. *Summary Report: 1975.* Doctorate Records File. Washington, D.C.: National Academy Press, 1975.

National Research Council. Office of Scientific and Engineering Personnel. *Summary Report: 1980.* Doctorate Records File. Washington, D.C.: National Academy Press, 1980.

National Research Council. Office of Scientific and Engineering Personnel. *Summary Report: 1989.* Doctorate Records File. Washington, D.C.: National Academy Press, 1989.

"New Carnegie Data Show Faculty Members Uneasy About the State of Academe and Their Own Careers." *Chronicle of Higher Education,* Dec. 18, 1985, pp. 1, 24–28.

Olivas, M. A. *The Dilemma of Access: Minorities in Two Year Colleges.* Washington, D.C.: Howard University Press, 1979.

Schwartz, H. "Affirmative Action." In L. W. Dunbar (ed.), *Minority Report: What Has Happened to Blacks, Hispanics, American Indians, and Other Minorities in the Eighties.* New York: Pantheon Books, 1984.

Stapp, J. "Minorities and Women: Caught in an Academic Revolving Door." *APA Monitor,* 1979, *10* (11), 14.

Suinn, R. M., and Witt, J. C. "Survey on Ethnic Minority Faculty Recruitment and Retention." Unpublished manuscript, Colorado State University, 1982.

U.S. Department of Commerce. Bureau of the Census. *General Population Characteristics, United States Summary.* Report PC 1-B1. Washington, D.C.: U.S. Government Printing Office, 1980.

U.S. Department of Commerce. Bureau of the Census. *Current Population Survey.* Washington, D.C.: U.S. Government Printing Office, 1990.

U.S. Equal Employment Opportunity Commission. Unpublished data, U.S. E.E.O.C. Higher Education Staff Information, EEO-6 data, Table 3, 1983. (Photocopied).

U.S. Equal Employment Opportunity Commission. Unpublished data, U.S. E.E.O.C. Higher Education Staff Information, EEO-6 data, Table 3, 1989. (Photocopied).

Vander Waerdt, L. "Affirmative Action and Tenure During Financial Crisis." *Journal of Law and Education,* 1982, *11* (4), 507–537.

HISAURO GARZA is associate professor in the Department of Chicano and Latin American Studies, California State University at Fresno.

The experiences of lesbian, gay, and bisexual faculty are examined in light of hostile campus climates. Suggestions are offered for building "communities of difference."

Enhancing Academic Communities for Lesbian, Gay, and Bisexual Faculty

William G. Tierney, Robert A. Rhoads

Jack, an assistant professor, comments on the problems of being gay: "You feel the pain of oppression, of having mirrored back to you everyday that you're different and that there are people who want to hurt you, and deny you basic human rights." Other faculty express similar feelings: Diane, a tenured faculty member, remains closeted because she fears she will be ostracized. Jeri feels that "coming out" is too big of a risk: "I never wanted to see myself leading a double life, but if I were out my supervisor could do some real damage to my life." A similar concern is voiced by John: "I'm concerned with the way people view me. I'm worried [about] what people will think, worried they will say, 'God, this person's a faggot.' " As these voices reveal, the campus environment is often hostile for lesbian, gay, and bisexual faculty.

The problems that lesbian, gay, and bisexual faculty face are harmful both to the individuals themselves and to their institutions; clearly, individual effectiveness is hampered when someone does not work in an organizational climate where he or she feels comfortable and appreciated. Accordingly, in this article our intent is twofold. First, we explore the extent of the problems faced by lesbian, gay, and bisexual faculty. We rely on a campuswide assessment project conducted at our institution, campus climate studies undertaken at other colleges and universities, and research efforts designed to come to terms with the extent of homophobia and heterosexism. Our second concern relates to how campuses might deal with these problems. We frame this latter discussion around the notion of "communities of difference" (Tierney, 1992) and offer suggestions about how academic communities might enhance cultural diversity, specifically with regard to lesbian, gay, and bisexual faculty.

Heterosexism and Homophobia

Herek (1980, p. 9) defined homophobia as "the general belief that homosexuality is sick, wrong, and disgusting, that it poses a danger to society (and should therefore be negatively sanctioned) and a threat to the individual (leading to an avoidance of contact with homosexuals)." Heterosexism is the fundamental belief that heterosexuality is the only legitimate sexual orientation. For lesbian, gay, and bisexual faculty fear is rooted in institutional cultures that reflect heterosexism and homophobia.

Heterosexism is typically more difficult to uncover than problems associated with homophobia since heterosexism is frequently buried in long-standing organizational structures and policies. Spousal benefit programs that favor heterosexual couples and deny benefits to lesbian, gay, and bisexual couples is one example of heterosexism. Violence against an individual because he or she is gay or lesbian is an example of homophobia.

Extent of the Problem

To their credit, a number of academic institutions have examined their campus climate for lesbian, gay, and bisexual students and staff. In general, the findings have been remarkably similar across all sites. For instance, at the University of Massachusetts-Amherst and at Rutgers University close to half of all lesbian, gay, and bisexual respondents reported that they had been verbally harassed (Nieberding, 1989; Yeskel, 1985). At Yale University and at UCLA over 50 percent of the lesbian, gay, and bisexual respondents reported fear for their safety (Herek, 1986; Shepard, 1990). Research projects that focused on student experiences reported similar findings (D'Augelli, 1989; Reynolds, 1989). The results of a campus-climate study conducted at our own institution—Pennsylvania State University—revealed that 64.3 percent of heterosexuals surveyed said they would be uncomfortable being alone with an individual who is openly lesbian, gay, or bisexual. Relatedly, 40 percent indicated they would be uncomfortable having an office mate who was openly lesbian or gay (Tierney and others, 1992).

One aspect of the Penn State campus survey was an open-ended question requesting the respondent to provide general comments regarding issues related to sexual orientation at Penn State. We here note some of the responses to underscore the problems lesbian, gay, and bisexual faculty face (La Salle and Rhoads, 1992):

> I feel too many resources are being devoted to minority groups. If you can't fit in, get the hell out!

I'm fed up with kowtowing to sexual perverts!

It is obvious that homosexuals are genetically inferior to heterosexuals, and therefore should be eliminated.

Gay and lesbian individuals are ill persons.

Of the more than eight hundred respondents who chose to provide comments, over half expressed some degree of resistance or intolerance. Keeping the preceding comments and the general results of the survey in mind, it is easy to see why so many lesbian, gay, and bisexual faculty choose to remain closeted. As Cathy, an untenured faculty member, noted, "Those of us who are in the closet survive through distance."

While many faculty remain for the most part silent, Pat Griffin, an associate professor of education at the University of Massachusetts-Amherst, has "come out" about her sexual identity: "Sure, I was nervous at first when I decided to tell people about my sexual orientation, but I'm reminded of a statement from the poet Audre Lorde, who says that if we wait till we're not scared anymore, we'll be speaking from our graves." Pat Griffin no longer lives in fear of being "found out." She has courageously proclaimed her sexual identity. She is no longer invisible. With these words in mind we shift our attention to the building of communities of difference.

Toward a Better Campus Climate

What possible actions might a postsecondary institution take to ensure that lesbian, gay, and bisexual faculty are more comfortable? We have offered examples that suggest both explicit and implicit problems. An individual who fears for his or her safety suggests that specific policies need to be created that ensure a safe environment. Yet a climate where people feel hesitant to speak about their private lives to individuals with whom they work paints a portrait of an institution that is not achieving its potential. That is, virtually all research on organizational culture argues that individuals are most effective in work settings where they are appreciated and affirmed. Attending to difference creates stronger academic communities. Thus, rather than focusing on reactive steps that try to respond to homophobic incidents on campus, we need to develop comprehensive proactive strategies. What follows is a thumbnail sketch of five remedial steps that some institutions already have undertaken:

Nondiscrimination. All institutions have statements about their commitment to certain ideals and the forms of discrimination they will not tolerate. The purpose of such statements is twofold. First, such commentary ensures that a person who is discriminated against because of his or her race, ethnicity, gender, or the like, has legal recourse. Second, statements of nondiscrimination are symbolic commentaries that point out institutional beliefs and values. In effect, we are saying that to discriminate against someone, for example, because of his or her color, is wrong.

To that end, colleges and universities should amend their institutional statements to include "sexual orientation" as a category for which they will not allow discrimination. Such an action provides fundamental protection for lesbian, gay, and bisexual faculty. Moreover, it points out that the institution has actively thought about this particular constituency, and it will not tolerate harassment against these individuals.

Equal Treatment. Lesbian, gay, and bisexual individuals do not ask for special treatment, and therefore they should not be asked to endure second-class citizenship. A community that honors differences among all of its constituencies ensures that everyone is treated fairly. Equitable treatment for lesbian, gay, and bisexual faculty begins when the academic community ensures that no one will be denied a job, a promotion, or some other good simply because he or she happens to be gay or lesbian.

Institutions also need to create policies pertaining to domestic partner agreements that extend to gay and lesbian couples the same rights and responsibilities given to heterosexual faculty. Domestic partner agreements have received increased consideration and support in the business world and in cities throughout the United States such as Madison, Wisconsin. Numerous corporations extend benefits to gay couples in the same manner as heterosexual couples; if colleges and universities want to develop equitable communities it is incumbent to follow the leadership shown in the business world.

In addition to domestic partner benefits, postsecondary institutions might want to reconsider definitions that pertain to "married faculty housing" or educational opportunities for one's spouse. Equal treatment suggests that the partner of a gay or lesbian faculty or staff member should be able to gain educational privileges or live in housing in a manner akin to a heterosexual's spouse.

Unequivocal Response to Acts of Intolerance. Free speech, academic freedom, and political correctness have become buzzwords on America's campuses. Institutional leaders seem particularly at a loss over how to respond to speeches, demonstrations, and newspaper articles that express obnoxious and repugnant attitudes. The conservative *Dartmouth Review* has perhaps garnered the most widespread publicity for creating a climate of intolerance, but such newspapers are found on many other campuses such as the University of Massachusetts and Duke University. These newspapers often have powerful conservative support. Indeed, at Penn State University a newspaper entitled the *Lionhearted*—which commonly attacks "homosexuals"—is funded by a member of the board of trustees.

Those campuses that have tried to limit free speech either have had their policies thrown out in court or the rules have had a harmful effect on what we have come to define as academic freedom. But no academic community should simply let racist, sexist, or homophobic commentary go unchecked as if these diatribes mean nothing. College presidents, their administrations, and faculty senates are often in a double bind because attacks are made or supported by powerful individuals such as a trustee or board member, or because they would rather not dignify the statements. The hope, it seems, is that such virulent commentary will simply go away. The National Gay and Lesbian Task Force (NGLTF), however, has gathered evidence that indicates that when homophobic comments are tolerated, violence against lesbian and gay people rises. One wonders, then, what might be the best way to combat hurtful speech and not infringe on academic freedom?

To paraphrase what Justice Oliver Wendell Holmes said more than a half-century ago, the way to fight bad words is with good words. When hate-motivated speech occurs on campus it is imperative that the institution's president swiftly speak out and denounce such talk. And because faculty look to their faculty senate for leadership, guidance, and support, it is also imperative that the chair or executive committee of the faculty senate speak out publicly and demonstrably in support of those individuals and groups under attack.

We emphasize that such comments need to occur swiftly, openly, and clearly. Hateful speech is like a fire: it will grow out of control if not responded to immediately, and it will continue unless it is met with clear resistance. Administrators and campus leaders can neither wait for the right moment to respond nor can they simply speak in private. The university community, and in particular lesbian, gay, and bisexual faculty, need and merit the support of leaders; silence or slow responses implicitly condone acts of intolerance.

Ironically, however painful intolerant language may be, institutional leaders have a unique opportunity to develop what we call a "teachable moment." Educational institutions should be dedicated to maintaining dialogue that fosters democracy and encourages students to engage in democratic citizenship. Accordingly, we do not suggest that free speech be limited, but a democratic community works only if those who have the voice to speak out use the authority and power of their office to do so and follow Justice Holmes's advice.

Research and Curriculum. An institution that honors diversity will encourage lesbian, gay, and bisexual studies. As with the statement of nondiscrimination, our point here is twofold. Faculty who have an interest in lesbian and gay scholarship ought to be able to undertake such studies without fear of retribution or discrimination with regard to promotion and tenure.

Obviously, the vast majority of lesbian, gay, and bisexual faculty are not found simply in one area of scholarship; as with any group, lesbian, gay, and bisexual faculty populate every academic discipline. A visible presence of lesbian, gay, and bisexual issues in the curriculum, research, and scholarship is a clear signal to faculty in all disciplines that such investigations are valued by the institution. Released time for course development, workshops on curricular integration, and a seminar series on "Lesbian and Gay Scholarship" are all viable ways to enhance understanding, dialogue, and support for lesbian, gay, and bisexual lives.

Acts of Empowerment. We address here perhaps the most difficult actions to undertake because they are the most personal. In the workplace individuals often do not like to confront a friend or colleague about personal issues. Consequently, homophobic jokes or comments are often made and go unchallenged. One of the clearest acts of support for lesbian, gay, and bisexual individuals can be those discussions in the workplace where we make known our displeasure about comments that ridicule, demean, or bring into question any particular group. Such a suggestion is of particular importance for academic leaders such as department chairs or college deans.

The vast majority of lesbian, gay, and bisexual faculty are closeted precisely because of unthinking commentary that goes unchallenged. Why risk "coming out" in a department where one's colleague has just made a joke about people with AIDS? How is it possible to bring one's partner to a party where a senior member of the department has offhandedly said that such pairings are "disgusting"? If we want people to work effectively, then they must be able to work in an environment where they feel welcome.

Further, we encourage those faculty who are closeted to rethink their invisibility. We fully realize the risks involved. We are not suggesting that individuals simplemindedly "come out," for we recognize that there are often good reasons to remain closeted. However, research has consistently shown that when individuals learn that a family member, friend, or colleague is gay or lesbian, homophobia decreases (Gentry, 1987; Wells and Franken, 1987). As Griffin notes (1992, p. 195), "Visible lesbian and gay educators provide colleagues, students, and parents with the opportunity to learn that their fears of and stereotypes about gay and lesbian teachers are not rooted in reality." Individuals in the "straight" community also need to realize the courage it takes for lesbian and gay people to risk such an act and offer support.

Conclusion

Difference, whether it be race, gender, class, or sexual orientation, is often difficult to confront. When we engage in discussions of difference, we are inevitably involved in actions where our most commonly held assumptions are brought into question. Our beliefs about how people should act may need to be redefined when we learn about other people. Our assumptions about what is right and what is wrong may need to be reconfigured when we hear other people's stories, hopes, and fears. And yet the enduring legacy of the United States is based not on monocultural attitudes, but on the quest to build a nation where respect for difference will not merely be tolerated, but honored.

Educational institutions have a unique role to play in building such communities. Colleges and universities do not merely prepare people to live in communities of difference; we live in those communities daily. The challenges that lesbian, gay, and bisexual faculty face will not be solved overnight, but the suggestions we have offered here highlight the truth that these problems can be overcome if we have the will and resolve to confront difference and engage in the work of building truly multicultural communities.

References

D'Augelli, A. R. "Lesbians and Gay Men on Campus: Visibility, Empowerment, and Educational Leadership." *Peabody Journal of Education,* 1989, 66 (3), 124–142.

Gentry, C. S. "Social Distance Regarding Male and Female Homosexuals." *Journal of Social Psychology,* 1987, 127 (2), 199–208.

Griffin, P. "From Hiding Out to Coming Out: Empowering Lesbian and Gay Educators." In K. Harbeck (ed.), *Coming Out of the Classroom Closet.* New York: Haworth, 1992.

Herek, G. M. "Attitudes Toward Lesbian and Male Homosexuals: A Refined Factor Analytic Approach." Paper presented at the meeting of the Western Psychological Association, Honolulu, Hawaii, May 1980.

Herek, G. M. "The Yale Sexual Orientation Survey: A Report on the Experiences of Lesbian, Gay, and Bisexual Members of the Yale Community." Unpublished manuscript, Yale University, 1986.

La Salle, L. A., and Rhoads, R. A. "Exploring Campus Intolerance: A Textual Analysis of Comments Concerning Gay, Lesbian, and Bisexual Persons." Paper presented at the annual conference of the American Educational Research Association, San Francisco, Apr. 1992.

Nieberding, R. A. (ed.). *In Every Classroom: The Report of the President's Select Committee for Lesbian and Gay Concerns.* Student Life Policy and Services Office, Rutgers University, 1989.

Reynolds, A. J. "Social Environmental Conceptions of Male Homosexual Behavior: A University Climate Analysis." *Journal of College Student Development,* 1989, 30 (1), 62–69.

Shepard, C. F. *Report on the Quality of Campus Life for Lesbian, Gay, and Bisexual Students.* Student Affairs Information and Research Office, University of California at Los Angeles, 1990.

Tierney, W. G. "Building Academic Communities of Difference: Gays, Lesbians, and Bisexuals on Campus." *Change,* 1992, 24 (2), 40–46.

Tierney, W. G., and others. *Enhancing Diversity: Toward a Better Campus Climate.* Report of the Committee on Lesbian and Gay Concerns, Pennsylvania State University, 1992.

Wells, J. W., and Franken, M. L. "University Students' Knowledge About and Attitudes Toward Homosexuality." *Journal of Humanistic Education and Development,* 1987, 26 (2), 81–95.

Yeskel, F. *The Consequences of Being Gay: A Report on the Quality of Life for Lesbian, Gay and Bisexual Students at the University of Massachusetts at Amherst.* Office of the Vice Chancellor for Student Affairs, University of Massachusetts, Amherst, 1985.

WILLIAM G. TIERNEY *is associate professor of higher education and senior research associate at the Center for the Study of Higher Education, Pennsylvania State University.*

ROBERT A. RHOADS *is a doctoral candidate in higher education and research assistant at the Center for the Study of Higher Education, Pennsylvania State University.*

The "model minority" myth for Asian Pacific Americans does not hold up well in higher education, where the academic pyramid for this group follows the general pattern of all minority groups and where tenure battles have begun to reverse the perception that Asian Pacific Americans will not fight for their rights.

Asian Pacific Americans in Higher Education: Faculty and Administrative Representation and Tenure

Don T. Nakanishi

The widely prevalent image of Asian Pacific Americans as a successful, model minority group serves to disguise their lack of representation and influence in major American social institutions, including higher education. Although there has been a dramatic increase in their enrollments at the undergraduate level in colleges and universities during the past decade (Hsia and Hirano-Nakanishi, 1989), the representation of Asian Pacific Americans at other levels of the academic hierarchy has been far less substantial. My own tenure case, which attracted considerable media attention during its three-year duration, demonstrates the unresponsiveness of the university hierarchy to racism so blatant even "so-called 'conservative' students" in campus fraternities and sororities at UCLA became involved (Omatsu, 1990a, p. 65). My attorney, Dale Minami, noting the wider implications of the case, stated that I "was a symbol of a New California where due to changing demographics, the majority of inhabitants would soon be people of color. . . . [M]any in the Ivory Tower, subconsciously or consciously, feared this" (Minami, 1990, p. 94). Because these demographic shifts are taking place so rapidly and with such widespread implications, greater policy and programmatic attention should be devoted to fair representation of and full participation by Asian Pacific Americans at all levels of higher education. My own protracted tenure battle has convinced me that Asian Pacific Americans must take a more active stand in our own behalf if we are to achieve fair representation in the academy.

In this discussion I will not review the details of my case, which are fully documented elsewhere (Omatsu, 1990b). Instead, I will focus on three widely prevalent myths or misconceptions regarding Asian American faculty and administrative representation and tenure. To do so, I will draw on several recent institutional studies and commission reports, as well as the experiences of over fifty professors from across the nation—over half of whom were Asian Pacific Americans and practically all of whom were women or scholars of color—who have contacted me since I received tenure in June 1989, and have sought my advice about what they should do in dealing with situations that resemble mine. Finally, I will summarize some of the political actions taken in my own tenure case, actions that unfortunately proved necessary although they challenged the myth of Asian Americans as the "model minority."

Misconceptions about Asian Pacific American Faculty and Administrators

The first misconception is that Asian Pacific Americans are well represented in college faculties and key administrative positions. This view is a simple and yet mistaken extension of the notion that Asian Pacific Americans are a successful minority, and that they are especially successful and talented in academics. Indeed, one might assume that since Asian Pacific Americans appear to be well represented in the freshman classes of many of America's leading colleges and universities (some have even charged that they are over-represented, particularly in the fall of 1991 when three University of California campuses—Berkeley, with 34 percent Asian American; UCLA, with 40 percent; and Irvine, with 51 percent—had freshman classes in which Asian Pacific Americans outnumbered whites), then by extension they must be equally well represented at other levels of these institutions.

The reality, however, is quite different. Like other minority groups and women in general, there is a substantial decline in the representation of Asian Pacific Americans as one moves up the academic pyramid from high school graduation to freshman admissions to graduate admissions and then to the ranks of faculty and administrators. At UCLA, for example, in 1987, the representation of Asian Pacific Americans followed a common downward pattern of declining representation (found at practically all major colleges and universities): 20 percent of the entering freshman class were Asian Pacific Americans, but they constituted only 10 percent of all entering graduate students, 6 percent of the nontenured faculty, and 4 percent of the tenured faculty (Minami, 1990). As I mentioned above, this pattern of diminishing presence in the academic hierarchy holds true not only for Asian Pacific Americans, but also for all other racial minority groups as well as women. On the other hand, at practically every major university in America, Whites reflect the opposite, upward pattern of increasing representation in the academic pyramid. For example, in 1987 at UCLA, Whites constituted 48 percent of the entering freshman class, 67 percent of all entering graduate students, 81 percent of all nontenured faculty, and 90 percent of all tenured faculty (Minami, 1990). Furthermore, Asian Pacific Americans in top administrative posts at UCLA and most major universities are practically nonexistent (Chan, 1989). Currently, only two of the top seventy-five administrators at UCLA are Asian Pacific American (Minami, 1990). Nationally, Asian Pacific Americans in administration constitute less than 1 percent of all administrators (Escueta and O'Brien, 1991).

To be sure, at most major universities it does not appear that Asian Pacific Americans are as grossly underrepresented in the faculty ranks as African Americans, Chicanos and other Latinos, and American Indians. In contrast to the situation of other minority faculty, there are usually some Asian professors on most college faculties (and usually more than the numbers of other minorities), where they usually are concentrated in specific fields like the sciences, engineering, medicine, or the teaching of Asian languages. However, this presence may be misleading, because often the professors in these fields are Asian foreign nationals who received a substantial portion of their higher educational training in Asian countries, rather than Asian Pacific Americans. For example, in one of the few empirical studies to address this issue, Stanford University (1989) found that in 1987 thirty-nine of the fifty-two tenure and nontenure line Asian faculty at its institution (75 percent) were born outside the United States, and thirty-one of these fifty-two Asian faculty members (60 percent) received their bachelor's degrees abroad. This situation, as the Stanford report pointed out, has several potentially unwarranted consequences for others in the campus community:

> While the Committee feels that all faculty are an asset to the University and the Stanford community, including all minority faculty by any definition, we also note that foreign-born and foreign-educated faculty members may not be as effective as role models for minority undergraduates, who are for the most part American-born. Students have described gaps in communication, especially in advising and counseling, arising from what they feel are the very different life experiences of minority faculty born and raised abroad. In such instances, mentoring—so important for the successful academic experience of minority students—can be strained [Stanford University, 1989, p. 19].

The second misconception is that Asian Pacific Americans do not face discriminatory or unfair employment practices in higher educational institutions. This view combines two widely accepted but false notions. First, it is an extension of the claim that Asian Pacific Americans have been fully accepted in American life, and that they no longer encounter either overt or covert racial discrimination that might limit their opportunities for social and professional advancement. The second underlying assumption is that colleges and universities are unique places of employment, that they are somehow more tolerant, more enlightened, more objective, and more open to new ideas and perspectives than institutions in the so-called real world, be they corporations, factories, or law firms, and that they are free of bias and subjectivity.

I do not believe that every Asian Pacific American faculty member faces racial discrimination. However, there is ample evidence from several studies, as well as the personal experiences of many individual professors who have publicly aired their situations, that Asian Pacific Americans from a variety of academic fields at different types of institutions across the nation have faced unusual and unfair treatment in their evaluations for tenure and promotions (Attorney General's Asian Pacific Islander Advisory Committee, 1988; Escueta and O'Brien, 1991; Minami, 1990). In the past few years the list of Asian Pacific Americans who have filed internal campus grievances or outside lawsuits in order to gain fair, unbiased, and equitable treatment for tenure and promotion has grown quite extensive and provides a brief glimpse of a potentially broader phenomenon. The disciplines represented in recent cases include business, medicine, architecture, biology and genetics, psychology, law, English literature, and my own field of education, to name just a few. These cases have involved major universities throughout the United States.

In higher educational institutions Asian Pacific Americans have encountered at least two major forms of unfair and potentially discriminatory treatment. First, like other minority and women scholars who pursue research in ethnic and gender studies, Asian Pacific American professors whose scholarship focuses on topics and issues concerning the historical and contemporary experiences of the Asian Pacific American population encounter the same misinformed, culturally disparaging, and often hostile reactions to and evaluations of their work by faculty colleagues. Ethnic and gender research that frequently confronts and challenges prevailing analytical perspectives and explores sensitive issues of racism and intergroup relations has yet to be fully accepted and embraced as important, relevant, or exciting subjects of study by many faculty members.

At the same time, Asian Pacific American professors have also encountered both covert and overt forms of racial discrimination. The significance of Professor Rosalie Tung's landmark Supreme Court lawsuit (*E.E.O.C.* v. *University of Pennsylvania*) is that the Court agreed with her attorneys and the Equal Employment Opportunity Commission that colleges and universities have no special privileges that should shield or protect them from fully disclosing relevant personnel review documents in a formal investigation of discrimination in employment. My own case also illustrates the absolute necessity of being able to have access to all original, unedited versions of tenure review documents rather than so-called redacted summaries that many universities like the University of California provide while pursuing internal campus grievances, as well as formal lawsuits. Although university officials claim that these edited summaries merely remove signatures, letterheads, and other identifiers to ensure confidentiality, they usually eliminate far more than that.

My case has some parallels with Professor Tung's because it involved high-ranking administrators of my professional school who worked in an unprecedented manner to influence and intimidate professors in my department and those who served on various independent reviewing committees to vote against my bid for tenure. The "redacted" summaries that I received completely eliminated all relevant information about the discriminatory actions of these individuals that was contained in my review documents. It was only because a dozen faculty members who sat on various reviewing committees in the multitiered tenure evaluation process had the courage to take the extraordinary action of breaking with the honored tradition of academic confidentiality, and to testify on my behalf in grievance hearings, as well as to provide me with the copies of unedited versions of my review documents, that we were able to lift the veil of discrimination in my case. And even in the seemingly enlightened and tolerant confines of a contemporary university community, there was ample evidence from several faculty witnesses that the top administrators in my professional school had referred to me privately on several different occasions as a "dumb Jap" or a "fat Jap." For three years, even after an independent academic senate grievance committee at my campus had ruled, on two separate occasions, that I had received unfair and biased treatment and that the top departmental official had engaged in "a deliberate attempt to deny tenure," the very highest ranking administrators of the university protected and supported this individual.

The third misconception is that Asian Pacific American professors who encounter problems in their employment or promotion are more inclined than other minority-group faculty to walk away and not contest an unfair denial of tenure or promotion. The decision to fight is a very difficult one, but as I indicated earlier, a growing number of Asian American professors across the nation and in different disciplines are asserting their rights and standing up for what they believe is right and proper—for their own sake, to be sure, in protecting their jobs or careers, or in gaining a fair and equal evaluation of their scholarly accomplishments, but also for the sake of other Asian Americans, other people of color, and women in all fields of employment, especially for those who are making their way up the academic pyramid and those who will be attempting to have meaningful and productive academic careers in the future. Asian Pacific Americans in general and Asian Pacific American professors in particular have been viewed stereotypically as passive and docile, and are expected (even more than the average assistant professor) to quietly fade away when a decision is made to deny them tenure.

However, I know from my own case and those of many other assistant professors with whom I have spoken that this kind of passivity is no longer appropriate. Many of us have come to the belief that it is our obligation to assert our rights and to stand up for what we believe—just as laborers did in an earlier period in Asian Pacific American history, and just as other Asian Americans have done and are doing in confronting glass ceilings in careers and fields that have been traditionally closed to Asian Pacific Americans. Without being overly rhetorical, there simply does come a time when one has to be the one that takes a stand. It is only by doing so that we can ever hope to advance in this society (Nakanishi, 1989).

Until recently the issue of Asian Pacific American faculty representation and tenure was not as forcefully or explicitly pursued by Asian Pacific American students, community leaders, or even other Asian American professors. I believe Asian Pacific Americans have paid a very heavy price for not fully advancing this issue. Both nationally and in the University of California system, Asian Pacific Americans have the lowest rate of tenure of all groups (Escueta and O'Brien, 1991). At the same time, as a special Asian Pacific American task force to California's state attorney general recommended in a recent report on Asian Pacific American civil rights issues, "Asian Pacific Islander Americans cannot continue to be represented predominantly as students within California's educational institutions. The poor representation of Asian Pacific Americans among the faculty and staff in those institutions can only perpetuate institutional biases that result in unfair admissions policies, financial aid decisions, academic curriculum planning and employment policies that are oblivious to the needs of Asian Pacific Islanders" (Attorney General's Asian and Pacific Islander Advisory Committee, 1988, p. 99).

The interest focused on my tenure case at UCLA during a three-year period and the support activities that surrounded it serve to highlight the extraordinary mobilization that the Asian Pacific American community of the 1990s is capable of mounting and willing to undertake to enhance the presence of Asian Pacific Americans in higher educational institutions, particularly in relation to their hiring and promotion as faculty and administrators. These actions share a number of features with the highly visible and effective lobbying and protest activities that were launched in relation to allegations concerning the possible use of admissions quotas for Asian Pacific American applicants to undergraduate colleges, reflecting this group's willingness to marshall support and resources to protect what they believe is their most important vehicle for social mobility (Nakanishi, 1989). I preface this list by noting that during the three years of this battle, my own department faculty voted five times to recommend tenure; and I won two internal campus grievances of discrimination. Prior to resolution of this case, the following actions occurred:

The *Los Angeles Times, New York Times,* and other media—especially the Asian American press—carried personal stories on my case.

Over 150 Asian American studies scholars from across the nation wrote letters of support.

Many members of the University of California Board of Regents called the highest ranking officials at the university about the case.

The entire Asian American congressional delegations from Hawaii and California wrote letters demanding that I receive tenure.

The Republican governor of California, at the urging of the Southeast Asian community in Orange County, called for tenure.

Tens of thousands of dollars were raised for a legal defense fund for my case.

An extraordinary array of major civil rights organizations, bar associations, chambers of commerce, and labor unions in the State of California wrote and endorsed resolutions demanding tenure.

UCLA students held three large rallies in support of my tenure on campus; the third rally received endorsements for the rally from over half of the California state legislature, the mayor of Los Angeles, every top Asian American elected official, a number of civil rights groups, and the undergraduate and graduate student body governments. It also attracted every television station in Los Angeles, along with reporters from all the city's newspapers.

Every major UCLA Asian American alumni donor demanded a meeting with top administrators to discuss my case.

Finally, the California legislature held up a $60 million appropriations bill to build a new business school building at UCLA, and requested a closed-door meeting with the chancellor, a meeting that ultimately resulted in an end to the struggle.

The extraordinary array of expressions of support that emerged on behalf of my own case reads like a handbook for political action. As my attorney noted, "Victory brought Asian Americans to a new understanding of our political power" (Minami, 1990, p. 81). The struggle also communicates the powerful resistance that Asian Pacific Islanders may encounter in their quest for equitable treatment. During my tenure case numerous doctoral students indicated to me that the outcome of my case would influence their decision to pursue doctoral research and careers in Asian American studies.

Recommendations

The representation and professional experiences of Asian Pacific Americans in the faculty and administrative ranks of American colleges and universities has not received sufficient policy or programmatic attention. As institutions grapple with an array of issues concerning ethnic and intellectual diversity, they should fully and positively consider the concerns of Asian Pacific American students, professors, staff, and administrators. I here offer several recommendations to assist institutions in their deliberations and planning activities:

1. Contact and work with a variety of national and regional professional organizations, representing a wide range of academic disciplines, to assist in the hiring and retention of Asian Pacific American faculty and administrators, and to gain a fuller understanding of the issues facing Asian Pacific Americans in higher education. These include, among others, the Association of Asian American Studies, California's Asian Pacific Americans in Higher Education organization, and Asian Pacific caucuses to professional associations like the American Psychological Association and the American Educational Research Association. Relevant organizations are listed in the November-December 1989 issue of *Change* magazine, which focused on Asian Pacific Americans.

2. Include Asian Pacific Americans as participants and as a focus of attention in all institutional planning activities and studies dealing with faculty diversity issues, and in efforts to augment the presence of scholars of color at your institution.

3. Be sensitive to the fact that Asian Pacific American faculty members from a wide range of disciplines have encountered both overt and covert forms of discrimination and prejudice in their professional careers, particularly in the consideration of tenure and promotion. In many cases, they represent the first scholars of color in a department, and may encounter difficulties that other pioneers have faced in entering new fields.

4. Take positive steps to recruit and train Asian Pacific Americans for academic and nonacademic administrative positions at your institution. Do not make unwarranted assumptions about their interest, or lack of interest, in becoming administrators, or their potential leadership talents.

5. Be cognizant of demographic projections, all of which suggest that the population of Asian Pacific Americans will continue to grow in all regions of the country. Issues about the fair representation of Asian Pacific Americans at faculty and administrative levels will continue to be compelling.

6. Recognize the diversity of Asian Pacific Americans, and the differences among them with respect to their participation at different levels of American higher education. Academic pipeline issues are still very important for the representation of all Asian Pacifics in certain fields, particularly the humanities, and for certain groups like Southeast Asians, Pacific Islanders, and Filipino Americans in practically all academic fields. Special attention should be paid to increasing the numbers of doctoral students from the latter three groups, and in increasing their opportunities for future professorial and administrative positions.

References

Attorney General's Asian Pacific Islander Advisory Committee. *Final Report.* Sacramento, Calif.: Office of the Attorney General, 1988.

Chan, S. "Beyond Affirmative Action: Empowering Asian American Faculty." *Change,* Nov.–Dec. 1989, pp. 48–51.

Escueta, E., and O'Brien, E. "Asian Americans in Higher Education: Trends and Issues." (American Council on Education) *Research Briefs,* 1991, 2 (4), 1–11.

Hsia, J., and Hirano-Nakanishi, M. "The Demographics of Diversity: Asian Americans and Higher Education." *Change,* Nov.–Dec. 1989, pp. 20–27.

Minami, D. "Guerilla War at UCLA: Political and Legal Dimensions of the Tenure Battle." *Amerasia Journal,* 1990, 16 (10), 81–107.

Nakanishi, D. "A Quota on Excellence? The Asian American Admissions Debate." *Change,* Nov.–Dec. 1989, pp. 38–47.

Nakanishi, D. "Why I Fought." *Amerasia Journal,* 1990, 16 (1), 139–158.

Omatsu, G. "Movement and Process: Building Campaigns for Mass Empowerment." *Amerasia Journal,* 1990a, 16 (1), 63–80.

Omatsu, G. (ed.). " 'Power to the People!' The Don Nakanishi Tenure Case at UCLA." *Amerasia Journal,* 1990b, 16 (1), 61–169.

Stanford University. *Building a Multiracial, Multicultural University Community: Final Report of the University Committee on Minority Issues.* Stanford, Calif.: Stanford University, 1989.

DON T. NAKANISHI is director of the Asian American Studies Center and associate professor in the Graduate School of Education at the University of California, Los Angeles. His successful three-year tenure battle is documented in the 1990 Amerasia Journal.

The results of an interview study that examined the career histories of twelve feminist and ethnic minority scholars are reported. Revealed are the challenges and struggles many of them have faced and the ultimate rewards and costs of dealing with gender and sociocultural issues within academia.

Challenges, Rewards, and Costs for Feminist and Ethnic Minority Scholars

Phyllis Bronstein

In the last fifteen years a number of new academic disciplines and subdisciplines have emerged, reflecting a more gender-balanced and multicultural worldview. While the level of acceptance of women's studies and ethnic studies as legitimate academic pursuits has varied across institutions, the overall body of scholarship has continued to grow. Interdisciplinary outlets for publication have emerged (such as *Signs, Women's Studies Quarterly,* and *Hispanic Journal of Behavioral Sciences*), as have outlets within specific fields (for example, in psychology, *Journal of Black Psychology, Psychology of Women Quarterly,* and *Women and Therapy*). As part of this movement toward the integration of gender and sociocultural issues into the curriculum, Kathryn Quina and I edited a book that provided information and resources about these issues for teachers of psychology (Bronstein and Quina, 1988). We invited scholars from all the main subfields of psychology to write chapters, whenever possible selecting people who were known for integrating gender and sociocultural issues into their teaching and for making those issues the focus of their research. When the book won an award from the Association for Women in Psychology (AWP), we were invited to present a program at the annual AWP conference. My task in this program was to describe the book's history: why we took on the project, and how it evolved.

As I thought about the process of putting the volume together, and the many fascinating phone conversations I had had with the contributors, I began to suspect that the history of the contributors themselves would be a far more interesting and informative topic for my AWP colleagues. What, after all, does it mean to develop an academic career in a nontraditional area, especially one that pertains to social and political change? Specifically, what does it mean to be doing ground-breaking work on gender and sociocultural issues as an integral part of one's academic career? I had the sense that embedded in many of the chapters of the volume was a *story* about what it means to be a leader in the transformation of our society—what the challenges are, and the rewards, and the costs. And I had the sense also, as I became better acquainted with the contributors, that their stories shared significant features. The data I then gathered to prepare for the program became the basis for this chapter, which examines some of the individual aspects and common themes of those stories.

Method

My approach was to conduct telephone interviews, in which I asked a series of open-ended questions about contributors' professional experiences (for example, "How was your focus on gender or multicultural issues received in your department and institution?"). I contacted twelve contributors from among the eighteen who had been in tenure-track academic positions for several years or more; levels ranged from assistant professor to full professor. For those who had been in such positions at more than one institution, I asked them to answer the questions in relation to the first position they had held—except for the question, "How are things for you now?" The subsample included seven ethnic minority faculty (four women and three men) who were African American or Hispanic, and five White women. Age, sexual orientation, and marital/parenthood status varied, as did religious background (for example, some of the White women and one woman of color were Jews). While most held primary appointments in psychology, a few held primary appointments in other departments or programs (for example, women's studies or African-American studies) or joint appointments with psychology. I did not interview any of the White male contributors: although some aspects of their teaching and research had included gender or sociocultural issues, those issues had not been the main focus of their career. The three areas covered were (1) how their institutions regarded and responded to them, (2) the impact they had on their institutions, and (3) the outcomes of the challenges they faced.

Results

One case, because it stood out so markedly from the rest, needs to be considered separately. The scholar in question was a White, gentile woman who had remained at the same university where she had received her first full-time, tenure-track appointment, and had risen to the rank of full professor. Her area of specialty was the psychology of women, and she was also very active on behalf of women at her institution, founding and participating in women's organizations and leading a women's network that dealt with women's problems on campus. Describing how she was regarded, she noted that she was highly respected, and indicated that her involvement with gender issues had always been viewed very positively; for example, the president, who was very pro–affirmative action, had appointed her to chair the university's affirmative action committee because "it wasn't doing enough." In addition, she was chair of her department, and had received rapid salary increases over the years, due to merit raises. She had married a university administrator before she had started her climb up the academic ladder, and she felt that being the wife of an administrator had helped prepare her for dealing with academic politics. Her ascent to political prominence on her campus had been a gradual one; she joined standard campus committees early on, and made connections with faculty in many departments, so that ultimately she had a wide base, and could deal with issues "behind the scenes and under the surface." Summing things up, she reported that she feels very satisfied with her own situation and career, and with what she has been able to do for other women.

This particular case stands out as a wonderful model of what can happen, but it also stands out because it is unique. What do the other eleven cases look like? It should be mentioned that all eleven people are productive scholars respected in their fields; that they all have been awarded major grants, published numerous articles and books, and won teaching awards. Over half have national reputations, and most of the rest are well on their way to achieving such recognition. All have been involved in research and teaching about ethnic and/or gender issues from early in their careers. Nine of the eleven were also involved in service activities in those areas—for example, developing ethnic and cross-cultural programs and training materials, being on affirmative action and ethnic studies committees, doing rape education programs, and doing outreach into ethnic minority communities.

Institutional and Departmental Responses. When I asked how their focus on gender or sociocultural issues was received in their department and institution, three of the eleven said that the response was mixed. All three reported that their departments (none of which were psychology departments) were interested in and supportive of their work, but that the university administrations were critical, unaccepting, and tended to withhold resources. Further, the administrations frowned on service involving the community, an activity viewed as an unworthy academic pursuit. Ethnic and women's studies were treated as "ghetto disciplines," and ethnically oriented journals were viewed as inferior publication outlets.

The other eight said that the responses of their departments and often their institutions had been largely negative. Here are some examples of how they felt their work was regarded:

From an ethnic minority man:

> They seemed supportive, but it was support that disappeared when you got close. There was verbal commitment to ethnic issues, but little follow-through. My department saw it as tangential, and tried to discount my work.

From a White Jewish woman:

> They said my work was tangential. I was told to cut my hair—that the graduate students wouldn't respect me with long hair like that. They didn't let me teach graduate students for several years, because I didn't cut my hair.

From an ethnic minority woman:

> On one level, it was received well, because of state and national policy. The university wants more diversity in the curriculum. But for some of the people in my department, there is the attitude that this is a stupid bunch of crap, peripheral, not real research. So there tends to be more lip service than support.

From another ethnic minority man:

> My work was viewed as service rather than research, because it was not "pure science"—I didn't use standardized measures (because they didn't apply to the population I was studying), and my research wasn't experimental or biological. It isn't "elegant" to try and look at real-life experience. They said, in effect, "Why waste time studying a population we don't have to worry about—indigent, powerless people? And it's not generalizable."

The most common criticisms were: (1) their work was tangential, peripheral; (2) it wasn't "real" or "pure" science; (3) it wasn't research at all—it was really service or teaching, and thus not as valuable (this referred to research that took place in classroom, community, or clinical settings); and (4) they weren't publishing in the "right" journals.

I then asked these scholars how they, personally, were regarded and evaluated by their institutions: Were they retained? Were they promoted? Were their evaluations affected in some way by their interest in gender or sociocultural issues? All eleven felt they had not been highly regarded in at least one institution at which they had worked, directly because of their commitment to gender and multicultural issues. Specifically, five were not rehired or were denied tenure; four fought and won attempts to deny them tenure or promotion; two were still fighting at the time of the interview; and three left before they came up for tenure to seek a more hospitable climate. This adds up to fourteen, not eleven, because some had struggles at more than one place. In addition, three had been or were currently involved in lawsuits against their institutions for gender or racial discrimination.

As people spoke about their lives in their departments, a theme that came up in nine out of eleven cases was isolation—in the work they were doing, as well as on a personal level:

> I needed to take blocks of time away, to be with others who were doing ethnic research.

> At my first job, I never could get anyone to be a coinvestigator on a grant proposal. Where I am now, I finally get asked a lot to be on other people's grants—but I have mixed feelings about it. Some just want a Hispanic, to better their chances [of obtaining funds].

> I've always been considered as different, not central, marginal. I got tenure, but still feel people don't like me. I'm perceived as a troublemaker. They write to the dean about me all the time.

Individuals' Impact on the Institution. On the other hand, not everything was seen as negative. When I asked them if they felt they had had an impact on their institution in the areas of gender, ethnic, and sociocultural concerns, all eleven had very positive things to say, often about more than one area. Seven spoke of their impact on students. For example:

> A lot of the minority students in my classes went on to med school and grad school, which makes me feel wonderful. It's very important to mentor students who will carry forward some of these issues, and increase person power.

> Every student who leaves my classes goes on to become a troublemaker in the rest of their classes, because they raise questions about research, and challenge the assumptions. So the faculty are getting more careful about what they say.

Four people spoke about their impact on their department or program, for example, restructuring the degree program in ethnic studies, or adding new courses. Three spoke of an impact on their institutions: affecting minority hiring, empowering students to push for change, and initiating multicultural programs. And five mentioned having had a positive effect on colleagues, in terms of the relationships they formed, the models they provided, and the resources they offered.

Outcomes of the Struggle: Winners, Losers, and Survivors. The next question asked how things were progressing for them now, in their current situation. Three of the eleven gave negative reports. One was going through a difficult tenure process while suing her institution. She has since written me that after having been denied tenure three times, fired, and then rehired with compensation, she has resigned her position, and left academia. Another was suing his former institution for denying him tenure, and the third one, though she has tenure, hates her situation and wants to leave.

For the other eight, however, the reports were more positive. Responses ranged from "Okay" to "Wonderful!"—with the more tentative ones coming from people who were feeling their way into new roles in their departments after winning tenure battles. Some of the comments were:

> I'm highly valued, and the women's studies program is strong, there is no discrimination against feminists, and I've been promoted rapidly [at the second institution].

> I don't have to worry about tenure any more—I do what *I* think is important.

> I have more power now. They have to listen to me because they want to keep me there [because of affirmative action requirements]. But they're not interested in my work.

> I am trying to transform my role from being perceived as an outsider and a troublemaker to being a leader and a catalyst for change. Having tenure and a big grant helps a lot.

Finally, I asked people if it had all been worth it. Were there benefits and gains, as well as costs? One person responded with a flat "No." She said, "What I went through was unnecessary. I should have had those things without the torture. I don't accept that it has to be that way." The other ten had a more positive view. This has changed for at least one of the respondents, the individual who recently resigned her position and left academia. Many spoke of their accomplishments in their teaching, and their enjoyment of it, as well as their connections with students. Some spoke of the impact their teaching and service activities had had on society, saying that this was important work. Others said that it was very rewarding to be doing research in an area that was close to their heart, and that could have an impact on what happens in the world. On a more personal level, several spoke of the friends they had made in being part of a national feminist network. Several spoke of what they had learned about White, male-dominated institutions—how to survive in them, or how to challenge them—and a number spoke of their own personal growth. For some, it seemed that they had discovered a deep moral commitment that went beyond their own individual career attainment:

> In my life, I decide what I'm going to do, and I do it. If you happen to decide to tenure me, fine. If not, fine. People are shocked—they don't know what to do with that. What will make a difference for me will be if I leave having made a difference. The end is not tenure. It's to make sure Black women who come through here will have a safer, kinder, gentler time when they come through.

> It *was* worth it. Women and ethnic minorities *have* to do it, no matter what it takes. I have access to change things more widely now, through my writing and speaking. I have more political influence in the university. I feel empowered because I survived. My worst fears were realized, and I survived.

> Yes, I would do it again, but I would be more assertive. Being a "good boy" brought me no points. Doing it over, I would be more politically savvy and vocal, and prepared to slug it out if necessary—and not be intimidated by *anybody*. The last thing we need is to try to please those people who are unsympathetic to minority views. We need to show them we are as smart as or smarter than they are, and can beat them at their own game. That's why mentoring is so important, and I'm happy to do that now.

> I made conscious political decisions as I went along. My status is higher in my own eyes. I am engaged in a serious battle at the highest level of American education [he is suing his institution]. If I win, there will be very serious changes in academia as a whole. For me to win would undermine the whole structure.

Discussion

One of the twelve scholars interviewed reported a highly positive professional history, in which she was well prepared for handling academic politics, and became a highly respected scholar and campus leader in promoting gender equity. All of the other eleven scholars interviewed reported that they had experienced racial and/or gender discrimination during their academic careers, often from both administration and department colleagues. And for ten of those eleven, their academic career advancement—and their academic survival—had at some time been in serious jeopardy. My interview did not ask them to speculate about the reasons for this discrimination. However, two main themes emerged from their responses.

The first is degree of "differentness." Academic institutions are micro-cosms of the larger society, and racism, sexism, classism, anti-Semitism, and homophobia are as endemic in institutions of higher learning as they are in society as a whole. Such attitudes may be even more pronounced in private institutions and research universities, because the key people running and influencing those institutions—administrators, faculty, boards of trustees, and wealthy donors—come mainly from the upper socioeconomic stratum, and are generally White, male, gentile, and heterosexual (see Bronstein, Rothblum, and Solomon, this volume). Thus there may be a strong impetus to maintain "traditional" values, standards, and curriculum, by which is meant, in part, maintaining the overt and covert structures that give access and preference to White, gentile, heterosexual males from financially privi-leged backgrounds. The treatment that the feminist and ethnic minority scholars in this study received supports this contention.

In general, the more "different" people were, in comparison with that mainstream model, the more difficult a time they had in their institutions, particularly on a personal level. Those who combined several "differentness" factors (such as female and ethnic minority and homosexual) reported experiencing the greatest amount of hostility from colleagues and/or the administration. In addition, it appears that for the women in the sample who came later to their first tenure-track position, age was another negative "differentness" factor.

The second theme, which relates to the first, is power. Feminist and ethnic minority scholars can present a threat to the status and privilege of White male faculty. What the respondents in this study universally reported was success with students: high demand and appreciation for the courses they taught, and for their services as advisers and mentors. Such responses from the "customers" in academic institutions have the eventual effect of shaping the curriculum, which means that those teaching the traditional offerings may find their services less valued and less in demand. For example, extra sections of the psychology of women course may need to be added because of undergraduate demand, while some of the more tradi-tional courses remain unfilled. In addition, mainstream male faculty may find that fewer graduate students choose to be involved in their research, so that their own scholarly productivity is reduced. Further, graduate student interests in feminist and multicultural issues may affect the direction of the program, so that the more traditional faculty may experience a loss of influence over course offerings, program requirements, and, in psychology, assignment of students to clinical training sites. And since faculty evalua-tions are usually made on comparative bases, White male faculty may feel that their own evaluations will suffer, in comparison with popular feminist and ethnic minority teachers. A number of respondents reported experi-ences suggesting that they were in fact seen as a threat to the existing power structure:

I have the highest teaching evaluations in the university—my courses are always overbooked—and I won the university's teaching award. Yet some of my colleagues have incredible hostility toward me. I've been pegged as a person who can only teach gender and culture, that I have problems teaching other things. And we have no minority grad students. When I argue that we should do something about that, it's gotten me a whole lot of flak.

They didn't want me to come up for full professor, because they didn't want two men who were coming up to have to compete with me. I had to fight for it.

I was the one person who would allow grad students to pursue interests in women and minority issues. I had the strongest group of grad students in the department, and no matter what people did to me, they formed around me and protected me, and kept me going. When I left, the department retaliated, and tried to throw out all the Black students.

Overall, the respondents felt that their efforts had had important impact, and had also, in many cases, contributed to their personal growth. For most, however, the costs had been high. All but one had changed institutions along the way, for reasons of politics or climate; two were currently in struggles to retain or regain their position; and three others were at best ambivalent about their current job situation. Several reported that they had experienced serious physical and/or mental health difficulties as a result of the stresses they had undergone. This latter fact is particularly noteworthy in light of the fact that our book was dedicated to six leading feminist scholars, all of whom died in middle age at the height of their careers, and that several other prominent feminist scholars have died prematurely since the book was published, one of whom was a contributor to the volume. One question that comes to mind is whether there is any other subfield in psychology with such a high mortality rate for prominent, nonelderly scholars. Another is whether there are ways to bring about changes in the discipline and in our institutions without suffering such high human costs.

The scholars in this study, along with growing numbers of others in academia with similar vision, courage, and determination, are having a major impact in their field. They are helping to reshape the discipline, moving it toward being representative of a much wider range of people—in terms of both the populations being studied, and the people doing the studying. Their impact is evident in the burgeoning body of scholarship that includes gender and sociocultural diversity, in new course listings, in new undergraduate and graduate programs, in textbooks, and in the public presentation of psychology. I recently received a letter from the author of a leading introductory text, detailing his use of our book as a guide for incorporating this scholarship into his textbook and his public television series (Zimbardo, 1992, personal communication). Psychology is changing, and when the students we are teaching today become tomorrow's academics, they will bring with them a more gender-balanced, multicultural perspective. At that point in time, being a feminist or ethnic minority scholar will continue to bring challenges and rewards, but the costs will have already been paid.

Reference

Bronstein, P., and Quina, K. (eds.). *Teaching a Psychology of People: Resources for Gender and Sociocultural Awareness.* Washington, D.C.: American Psychological Association, 1988.

PHYLLIS BRONSTEIN is associate professor of clinical psychology at the University of Vermont. She has done research on women's professional advancement and is editor of the book Teaching the Psychology of People: Resources for Gender and Sociocultural Awareness.

*Women and minorities who make unadaptive starts in the professoriate
evidence a series of reliable turning points early in their career,
typically within their first few semesters on campus. Origins of such
career fault lines begin with deficits, notably in regard to preestablished
mentoring and social networks. The simple nature of these turning
points also implies strategies for preventing or reversing the
disappointing and marginalizing beginnings so common for
nontraditional new hires.*

Early Turning Points in Professorial Careers of Women and Minorities

Robert Boice

Why has a growing chorus of dissatisfaction and documentation failed to
improve the lot of women and minorities in the professoriate (Blum, 1991)?
Appropriately, we place much of the blame on sexism and racism: academe
has provided a chilly climate for these nontraditional faculty members
(Rothblum, 1988). But we could also fault ourselves for not yet identifying
the practical interventions most likely to help women and minorities fare
better in professorial careers.

My own efforts with marginalized professors aim more at the second
issue, of finding ways to hasten the reversal of tradition. I base this chapter
on the assumption that we need to know more about where careers of
nontraditional faculty go off track and how to prevent derailments. Specifically, I present three steps of inquiry that: (1) locate the reliable and common
turning points of women and minorities in troubled careers; (2) show how
quickly and needlessly crucial events occur for these marginalized newcomers; and (3) suggest the potential ease and economy of preventing these
negative turning points.

To map the career patterns of nontraditional and traditional newcomers
(that is, fix the sequence of turning points associated with lasting patterns
of success or marginalization), I rely, first of all, on a long-term, reflective
strategy from cognitive science for recovering reliable memories of turning
points in careers. As I use this procedure, it immerses recent hires in
repeated sessions of recall over periods of at least a year. In contrast, other
studies of faculty members draw career maps from single, spontaneous
recollections of events that determined directions. Second, I focus on faculty

careers during what biologists might call the primary critical period, the brief window of time during which newcomers either imprint on appropriate social models or else face a peripheral and perilous existence. And, finally, I draw on observations of a group of exemplary women and minorities to gain insights about what can help their counterparts fare better in academe (Boice, in press). As a rule, research on women and minorities tells us too little about success.

Three Study Questions

I began my investigation of career turning points by asking whether clear negative marker events occur predictably for faculty and, if so, when. I then asked whether career turning points differed noticeably for women and minority faculty and, finally, whether the career experiences of highly successful women and minority faculty would give insights as to how negative turning points could be prevented. In what follows, I describe the research procedure and report on the patterns I observed.

When Do Negative Turning Points Occur? Customarily, we look on faculty careers in terms of developmental stages that last as long as, say, the six or seven years leading to tenure decisions. From these global accountings previous researchers have drawn conclusions about what might have facilitated careers, usually in terms of missed opportunities for resources and rewards throughout professorial lives (Blackburn and Havighurst, 1979). But these inquiries tell us little about early experiences that might set lasting patterns of marginalization. There is but a single precedent based on thoroughgoing research: we already know that initial habits and successes in writing productivity are difficult to reverse (Creswell, 1985).

By the time I began my own efforts at career mapping I had seen signs of early turning points in a decade of research with new faculty (Boice, 1992b). And I had happened onto Perkins's (1981) methodology for retrospective thinking aloud protocols. I modified his strategies (which he uses for uncovering key thoughts and feelings that accompanied creative acts) into a series of patiently conducted reconstructions of points-of-no-returns in careers. Briefly, I trained individuals to recall and describe pivotal events since coming to campus; subjects carried on a train-of-thought narrative as I listened, took notes, and occasionally asked for clarification or summarization. As we carried out the recollections in repeated sessions during which all accounts began again from scratch, I was able to elicit increasingly refined and reliable reconstructions of central events in what individual participants and I came to agree were the most crucial of turning points. I present details of this methodology elsewhere (Boice, in press).

With a minimum of direction and a lot of practice, the participants in these studies learned to move past superficial explanations of career events to what Perkins calls "reporting." The following excerpts from one new faculty member illustrate the difference between explaining and reporting:

> [*Explaining*]: I reacted defensively because there was no way to be ready for the sexism that I encountered here. The jokes about my pregnancy showed me that my colleagues were not ready to deal with women's issues.

> [*Reporting*]: I can recall the moment, maybe a point of no return, when I felt helpless here . . . that I would never be accepted by the men in my department. I cheerfully and spontaneously joined a few of them for lunch, by just asking if I could join them. I soon felt unwelcome. I suspected that I had interrupted something that they didn't want to continue in my presence. I thought to myself: "This feels like being a graduate student. I'm not their equal. I'm not really welcome. This is how it's going to be here . . . with you, the little girl, on the outside looking in."

With repeated practice at listing the most crucial of career events that shaped their destiny as fledgling professors, all these subjects spontaneously trimmed their lists to three, four, or five turning points over the yearlong course of our investigations. My directions to participants were limited to reminders about the value of minimizing interpretations and of sticking to events with the greatest likely influence on their careers.

The first and most essential finding of my inquiries with retrospective thinking aloud protocols was that turning points came with surprising— often devastating—speed. All but a few new faculty members eventually cited experiences during their initial semesters that promised to have lasting influences on their careers.

Even where I tracked new faculty into their sixth and seventh years with once-a-semester interviews, the reliability of listing the same early turning points held fast. So did reports of anger over other discouraging beginnings. That is, while events beyond the second year often exacerbated poor be- ginnings, they rarely changed already established directions. Points of no re- turn not only appeared rapidly but they also seemed to occur irreversibly.

To provide another check for the consistency of early turning points reported by faculty, I studied midcareer faculty with the same retrospective thinking aloud procedure with repeated sessions of recall and listing of crucial events (Boice, 1992a). Once experienced at recalling thoughts and feelings, the most disillusioned of midcareer faculty ($N = 33$) listed a reliably similar set of negative experiences and interpretations that had occurred during their first years on campus. Their experiences fell into broad catego- ries: (1) collegial isolation, (2) collegial disapproval, (3) self-doubts about competence, and (4) feeling victimized and suspicious. The most telling of turning points seen from the vantage of midcareer virtually duplicated the timing of similar experiences for the samples of unadapted new faculty. Evidently, turning points do happen early on and then endure.

Do Events Surrounding Points-of-No-Return Distinguish Women and Minorities from White Men? When I began to report on the maps of the early careers of new faculty in colloquia and publications, some listeners and readers, all of them men, made a similar supposition. They imagined that I had depicted a degree of collegial isolation, lack of resources, and slow progress in domains such as teaching where men were no less disadvantaged than women and minorities. My colleagues were probably mistaken. The incidence of subtle discriminations, of lesser social supports from sources such as chairpeople, and of stresses and unmet expectations was apparently greater for women and minorities than for White males in these samples.

To answer this question even more systematically, I undertook a series of comparative inquiries beginning with traditional methods; at first, I relied on repeated interviews about the experiences and plans of new faculty ($N = 42$ women, including 7 of color; 42 White men plus 4 of color) coping with two large campuses, one a comprehensive and one a research university (Boice, in press). Interviews usually continued for six successive semesters. Women's responses stood out on many dimensions: First, they, far more than their male counterparts, valued teaching but were more put off by negative experiences as teachers (for example, seeing colleagues as disinterested in discussing teaching; sensing that students would only accept them if they were entertainers; realizing that male students treated them less generously than they would male professors). Second, they, more than White men as new faculty, sought out collegiality, especially friendship, but ended with far fewer opportunities for useful mentoring or collaboration in research or teaching. Perhaps women are less comfortable with the hierarchical nature of mentoring than men are (M. Svinicki, personal communication, Aug. 1992). And third, they, compared to males, reported more instances of illness and of debilitating anxiety while teaching or writing.

But there were disturbing confounds in these inquiries. Because women were far more disclosive in these somewhat open-ended interviews, their contribution to the sample of experiences more than doubled the input of men. The result probably distorted accounts of new faculty lives. Moreover, even with what I had learned about women as new faculty, the correctives for their complaints remained somewhat vague. For example, it was obvious that women were less tied into the most important kinds of support networks. But how, beyond offering them participation in the same mentoring programs as men (Boice, 1992b), could we overcome this deficit? To answer this question, I moved to another inquiry.

In a more-involving probe with the same cohorts of newcomers, I used a detailed assessment device, the New Faculty Faring Index (NFFI; Boice, in press). The NFFI evaluates progress of new faculty over four general categories: (1) immersion in career and campus activity (for example, interacting with students outside classrooms and participating in campus activities such as choral groups); (2) regimented habits of working (for instance, regularly spending at least two hours a week on scholarly writing); (3) self-management (for example, evidencing optimism on a standardized analysis of spoken or written "discourse"); and (4) social management (for instance, spending as much time at collegial networking, on and off campus, as at writing, and arranging adaptive mentoring that includes support, advice, and networking).

The NFFI requires direct observations by faculty development practitioners acting as classroom and office visitors, as interviewers of chairpeople and other senior colleagues, and as analysts of archival materials (such as manuscripts completed, student evaluations of courses, and renewal decision reports). One advantage of this scrutiny lies in the fact that new faculty themselves were not always the best judges of how they were progressing. Through these multiple sources, I found that:

Women evidenced a far higher incidence of blocking at writing and of procrastinating in general

Minorities were especially likely to be perceived as separatists who spurned mentorship and sponsorship advances from senior colleagues

Both women and minorities failed more generally to take advantage of opportunities to enlist undergraduates as research assistants or colleagues as collaborators

Both of these marginalized groups were more often seen by colleagues as identifying too closely with teaching and students, to an extent that would undermine their careers as researchers and scholars.

These NFFI results provide the first systematic ratings of new faculty faring, indices that in fact predict survival and satisfaction for new hires. My own ongoing reanalyses of samples of new faculty whom I have tracked for years (Boice, 1992b) corroborate the link between high scores on the NFFI and other indexes of success such as retention, promotion, and career satisfaction. Moreover, each of the twenty rating items of the NFFI suggests remedies for low scorers. Finally, the NFFI, by evidencing positive connections between all its dimensions, reminds us that teaching does not occur in a vacuum: as a rule, new faculty who fared poorly across the measures of teaching (for example, student evaluations, classroom comfort, involvement with students) performed just as problematically in areas such as collegiality and scholarly productivity.

On the other hand, the NFFI falls short of specifying economical correctives because it pictures shortcomings for women and minorities in a way that suggests almost too many remedies for practical implementation. Thus I found myself looking for a way to simplify the picture.

The next step of investigation relied again on data from the retrospective thinking aloud protocols, this time focusing on samples of notably unadapted new hires ($N = 21$). The results revealed the following sequence of crucial experiences for the most unadapted of White men as new faculty: (1) feeling deceived about resources for research during hiring; (2) realizing that the busyness of teaching would discourage publishing and career goals; and (3) giving up on colleagues as potentially fair. For unadapted women, the composite list of turning points differs somewhat. The crucial experiences for unadapted women include: (1) feeling treated as second-class citizens during recruitment; (2) feeling neglected and unsupported by colleagues; (3) discovering that students demand pandering; and (4) deciding that the work is too stressful to be worthwhile. And, finally, the sequence of crucial events for minority women looks like this: (1) discovering that loneliness is complicated by the prospect of never feeling a part of a department and campus; (2) feeling overwhelmed with fears of failure and with helplessness about remedying personal shortcomings such as language problems; and (3) deciding to deal with students and colleagues by becoming tough and quiet.

In some ways the pattern of early failure is similar across all three groups. Alienation occurred quickly, usually within the first semester or two. Decisions to give up on careers, to just muddle along or to leave campus, came shortly thereafter. In other ways, though, the pattern does distinguish women and minorities from White males. Unadapted men felt put off and forced to withdraw from competition by a combination of not getting the resources they saw as necessary to compete as researchers, by perceiving teaching as a distraction that kept them from publishing as much as they had hoped, and by having colleagues who seemed to treat them unfairly.

Women as new and unadapted faculty, in contrast, reported being derailed more by personal events for which they often felt responsibility: by social slights, by collegial isolation, by rejections from students, and by the stresses of marginalization. Thus, the issues for men and women fit predictable patterns, with the former caring mostly about competition and fairness, and the latter caring more about cooperation and affiliation. In contrast, the profile of early career events for unadapted minority women heightens the contrast with White men, as though the pattern had been exposed to more intense lighting. These women not only felt isolated and likely to fail; their decision to react with toughness suggests that they could see no hope of improvement or flourishing in academic careers.

This identification of early turning points suggests practical, economical ways of preventing them and the time for doing so. Moreover, these findings suggest that crucial events generally differ for men and women. An example of an early turning point for women illustrates a timely intervention: once we appreciate the special pressures experienced by women in response to student demands for entertainment and easy grading, we could begin to shape our instructional development programs for new faculty to deal with this and other immediate needs (as opposed to more typical emphases such as encouraging newcomers to deemphasize lecturing in favor of discussions). If we cannot help our new hires find classroom comfort and acceptance, plans to train them in cooperative learning strategies may be idealistic.

What Can Early Career Maps of Exemplary Women and Minorities Tell Us? We may be able to learn the most about how to prevent negative turning points by studying the protocols of exemplary new faculty. A glance at the modal pattern of crucial events for thirty-one new faculty labeled as quick starters (Boice, 1992c) shows why. For these new faculty (whose chairpeople judged them clear successes in terms of teaching, writing, and collegiality), gender or race made little difference in first impressions. The earliest crucial event was almost always occasioned by coming to campus with a social network and with mentoring already in place. The actual turning point came when these new hires recognized that success on campus had been essentially prearranged: these new hires, because of prior social connections and memberships in extended groups of researchers with similar interests and academic heritages, were assured collaborations and friendships on their new campuses as a matter of course. This realization was not, however, something publicly discussed or apparent to less-advantaged newcomers.

Beyond this first turning point for exemplars, though, success patterns again reflected predictable gender differences. Women, on the one hand, were more affected by affiliative experiences—for example, finding comfort with teaching and acceptance from students led them to believe that they had chosen the right careers. And they, more than exemplary males, reported the conscious decision to treat problems as useful challenges (for example, unsophisticated undergraduates were seen as individuals who would respond with special gratitude to opportunities for apprenticeships with their professors; fatigue was seen as a reminder to make time for exercise). Men, as before, experienced events connected with competitive success as pivotal: their second turning point was a matter of gaining acceptance for an important grant or manuscript that provided them status and resources. Their third crucial experience was the opportunity to become consultants or committee members in ventures that took them away from campus and gave them financial security and prestige. Here, at least, the Old Boy network continued to work along traditional lines.

There are, I believe, two main messages in these chartings of quick starters. One reinforces the notion that negative turning points can be prevented. Nothing, evidently, will help ensure a strong start more than prearranged networks of support and mentoring. Yet few campuses have implemented programs to provide such networks, despite their practicality, low cost, and desirability. The second point is that we would have to stretch our resources very little to provide more consistently positive experiences during the hiring process. In my ongoing studies of women and minorities who leave academe for other careers, I find repeated confirmation of this observation. For instance, once they see the comparatively humane and supportive initiations offered in corporate settings, women and minorities marvel that they originally opted for the social Darwinism of academe.

Obstacles and Implications

What will keep us from acting to prevent the rapid and irreversible marginalization depicted here? One thing may be the seeming sexism and racism in traditional demands for faring well in the professoriate. I find that women and minorities understandably wonder about the worth of mimicking White male values such as competitive publishing. They ask, "Wouldn't it make more sense to count presentations of research at conferences that allow for face-to-face interaction as much as publication in exclusionary and male-dominated journals?"

A second obstacle is the great fly wheel of tradition. Exum (1983), as a Black and a gay, saw that academe, because it aims for societal and not economic goals, moves very slowly and conservatively. He recognized that senior White men who set policies see themselves as enlightened protectors of intellectual standards, and are therefore likely to respond indignantly to suggestions that they move too slowly in recruiting and retaining women and minorities into optimal careers.

The third obstacle is the habit of not looking in the right places for interventions, of not considering that we could redirect the course of many faculty careers away from marginalization with but a few civil and inexpensive changes. We should, in my view, be most optimistic about prospects of overcoming inertia in this dimension given its apparent simplicity.

In the end, though, preventing the early turning points that derail the careers of our nontraditional newcomers will be neither simple nor inexpensive. Making the environment to which women and minorities adjust healthier and fairer could necessitate changing the academy itself. It would mean building supports, no matter how uncomplicated in themselves, where almost anyone who qualifies for entry into the professoriate would likely thrive. The result would be a democratization that could challenge the most cherished of traditions: above all else, academe values demonstrations of brilliance that occur with little obvious effort or assistance. The real question may concern our willingness to pay the price for equality of opportunity—that is, a tempered definition of excellence, one less tied to unaided demonstrations of individual brilliance and to elitist practices that disable professors who need affiliation and coaching to succeed.

References

Blackburn, R. T., and Havighurst, R. J. "The Academic Career as a Development Process." *Journal of Higher Education*, 1979, *52*, 598–614.

Blum, D. E. "Environment Still Hostile to Women in Academe, New Evidence Indicates." *Chronicle of Higher Education,* Oct. 9, 1991, pp. A1, A20.

Boice, R. "Midcareer, Disillusioned Faculty." Paper presented at the American Association for Higher Education Meetings, Chicago, Apr. 1992a.

Boice, R. *The New Faculty Member.* San Francisco: Jossey-Bass, 1992b.

Boice, R. "Quick Starters: New Faculty Who Succeed." In M. Theall and J. Franklin (eds.), *Effective Practices for Improving Teaching.* New Directions for Teaching and Learning, no. 48. San Francisco: Jossey-Bass, 1992c.

Boice, R. "New Faculty Involvement of Women and Minorities." *Research in Higher Education,* in press.

Creswell, J. W. *Faculty Research Performance: Lessons from the Sciences and Social Sciences.* Washington, D.C.: Association for the Study of Higher Education, 1985.

Exum, W. M. "Climbing the Crystal Stair: Values, Affirmative Action, and Minority Faculty." *Social Problems,* 1983, *30,* 301–324.

Perkins, D. N. *The Mind's Best Work.* Cambridge: Harvard University Press, 1981.

Rothblum, E. D. "Leaving the Ivory Tower: Factors Contributing to Women's Involuntary Resignation from Academia." *Frontiers,* 1988, *10* (2), 236–241.

Robert Boice is professor of psychology at the State University of New York at Stony Brook, where he also directs the Faculty Instructional Support Office.

National Institutes of Health programs supporting minority students in biomedical research offer an effective model of mentoring that can be replicated across the academic disciplines.

"I Can Do It": Minority Undergraduate Science Experiences and the Professional Career Choice

Robert M. Hoyte, Jonathan Collett

> I was very shy and I spoke with an accent. . . . I remember the first scientific meeting I attended was an MBRS national meeting in New Orleans. I saw a lot of people like myself there who also spoke with an accent. I thought as long as they can do it I can do it too. It was an extremely good experience to be able to interact with other students who were also doing research.

Dr. Maria Alvarez is more confident now, more articulate, with just a trace of an accent. But as a lecturer removed from the tenure track she certainly does not have the kind of security she should probably be given because of her status as a member of a rare species: a minority scientist. A Hispanic woman with a Ph.D., teaching and coordinating freshman labs in the Biology Department at the University of Texas at El Paso, she is ideally situated to spark an interest in science in her students, particularly women and Hispanics. In just such a way her own interest was sparked by a teacher she took as a role model at the same university when she was an undergraduate.

It will take many Dr. Alvarezes if we are to reverse the projected shortage of scientists in our country, including the scientists in academe. The college-age White population is expected to decline by about 20 percent, or some 868,000 students, by 1998 (measured from a 1979 baseline). Thus a more equitable representation of minorities among faculty becomes all the more important (Solmon and Wingard, 1991, p. 23). Added to this general decline are declines in the number of science baccalaureates earned and in the percentage of science doctorates awarded to Americans (Project Kalei-doscope, 1991a). The greatest population growth will occur for Hispanics and Asian Pacific Americans. Indeed, these two groups have already experienced the largest gains in science degrees, although Hispanics are still badly underrepresented (Carter and Wilson, 1992). African Americans lost ground in undergraduate and graduate degrees overall in the 1980s. The decline among African Americans is even more precipitous in science degrees (Project Kaleidoscope, 1991a).

To fill the critical shortage of scientists, including scientists in the professoriate, new approaches to science education must be implemented for all students at all levels, but especially for minority and women students. As Dr. Alvarez's story suggests, this education must include confidence building, incentives, role models, mentoring, and other features not normally considered in the traditional undergraduate science curriculum.

The lack of role models is a particularly acute factor that mitigates against minority students conceiving of academic careers because they have very little experience in their communities, much less in their own families, of people who have been successful in academe. Those students who make it to college will, of course, come into contact with such successful persons, but whether students see themselves following in a professor's footsteps may depend on the nature and extent of contact with that professor. The ideal situation occurs when the student has close contact with the professor in a working intellectual relationship. This type of relationship is the recognized norm in the way graduate students are trained in most disciplines, especially at the predoctoral level. It is unusual, however, for this type of close intellectual mentoring to occur at the undergraduate level.

"I'm going to be sure that my work as a doctor always includes teaching," says Dr. Stanley Parker, a radiologist who teaches and does clinical work and research at the University of Iowa College of Medicine. "All of my important role models have been teachers." Dr. Parker still travels back to the southern Black college from which he graduated to encourage students to consider a career in medicine—and teaching.

NIH Support for Minority Students in Biomedical Research

What Drs. Alvarez and Parker have in common and what helps to explain how they got to their present positions, as both would attest, was their participation in a federally sponsored program in the sciences for minority students. The National Institutes of Health (NIH) recognized very early the potential value of faculty mentors for undergraduates by establishing the Minority Biomedical Research Support (MBRS) and the Minority Access to Research Careers (MARC) programs. Begun in 1972 and 1977, respectively, these programs were designed to increase the numbers and quality of minority students pursuing careers in the biomedical sciences.

The MBRS program supports peer-reviewed faculty research projects at designated institutions that are committed to minority education. It uses a three-pronged approach in pursuing its objective: it promotes the professional development of faculty on minority campuses which usually have scarce or nonexistent resources for research; it aids the development of a research infrastructure at the institution; and it supports student participation in research projects at both the undergraduate and graduate levels. Typically, students work on a defined research investigation part-time during the academic year and full-time during the summer. They receive compensation sufficient to cover their academic and personal needs, thus eliminating the need for off-campus employment. The MARC program is an honors training program that operates in a similar way to MBRS, except that it does not provide direct support of research. Instead, it directly supports students with tuition and stipend funds and also supports summer research experiences away from the campus at a major research center.

Faculty Mentor Undergraduates. The laboratory work of Karlene Bryson, a junior at SUNY College at Old Westbury, is a good example of an MBRS chemistry research project. It involves the chemical synthesis of radioactive analogs of the steroid hormones for medical diagnostic purposes. Bryson's research project is to carry out a multistep synthesis that requires the chemical and physical characterization of the product of each step. This synthetic work is a direct application of principles learned in the sophomore organic chemistry course she began to take at the start of her project.

While her professor-mentor is available for consultation and follows her work closely, he is not in the lab all the time. She is expected to develop increasing levels of independence as the work progresses, not simply to follow instructions, but to exercise judgment in seeing the project to its conclusion. Bryson characterizes her increasing sense of confidence in these words: "And then you start to think, I'll never be like him, but then you get into the lab and you actually come to say, 'Professor, I think this should be this way, wouldn't it be better?' And then if he says yes, you say, 'Wow, I'm really going places.' " The development of independence and the exercise of judgment, prerequisites for good scientific research, are characteristics that the MBRS program seeks to develop in all areas of a student's life.

Close personal contact with the faculty supervisor and other participating students promotes self-confidence and a sense of belonging. Another MBRS student, Marjorie Bonhomme, describes her new level of confidence: "I've gotten to the point where I'll do something and I'm not afraid to mess up. Before I didn't want to do anything at all, not even take one step, but now it's OK to mess up, . . . because you tried and at least you're going to be acknowledged because you tried."

In addition, MBRS and MARC students travel to an annual national symposium, where they may present their research results among peers. They are also encouraged to attend a national or even international professional meeting. Dr. Frank Perez, a research associate at Penn State, recalls how important the national symposia were for him: "To interact with so many members of underrepresented groups from around the country was a very uplifting experience, particularly when you have several hundred at different levels. We're talking about faculty members, university administrators, and students. It was an excellent opportunity to develop a network and there were ample role models. . . . As a body, that is a very powerful force. It sends out a very positive message." Karlene Bryson will go to her first symposium next year, but she already knows how to put the experience to good use: "You meet people from industry and graduate schools. When you come back here you say this is what I have to do because I know what those grad schools require. When they say we want well-rounded students, if you're not well-rounded, you come back here and you have another year to get well-rounded."

Program Results. About 1,500 MBRS and 600 MARC students are chosen each year. As of 1990, approximately 16,000 minority students had participated in the two programs. About 1,300 have gone on to earn doctoral or professional degrees, and several hundred more are still in graduate school. Originally established on campuses where minorities are a majority, such as historically black colleges and universities (HBCU's) and predominantly Hispanic institutions, such as the campuses of the University of Puerto Rico, MBRS and MARC have been extended to a number of predominantly White institutions with sizeable populations of minority students. In 1990 101 campuses were awarded grants. A 1985 study (Garrison and Brown, pp. 57–58) showed gains in the percentages of minority majors in the biological sciences at MBRS and MARC institutions well above national averages for African Americans and Hispanics.

The most impressive figures relate to the impact of MBRS and MARC on the production of minority Ph.D.'s. In the five-year period 1985–1989 Hispanic and African American MBRS students received 101 Ph.D.'s in biology and chemistry, or 17.5 percent of all doctorates in those fields earned by Hispanics and African Americans (National Institutes of Health, 1992). MARC produced 31 Ph.D.'s in that period. Together, the two programs already account for almost a quarter (22.9 percent) of the total Ph.D. production of African Americans and Hispanics in biology and chemistry, and this percentage is growing rapidly as more program students enter the pipeline and work their way through graduate school. Program participants have not been thoroughly tracked along their career paths, so of course it is possible that participants' decisions at various stages may be the result of influences other than the MBRS or MARC experience. But the case can certainly be made that MBRS and MARC are to a large extent responsible for

African American men, particularly, holding their own in Ph.D.'s in the life sciences and showing a slight gain in the health sciences from 1975 to 1990. These results come in spite of the precipitous decline of more than 50 percent among African American men in all Ph.D.'s earned during the same fifteen-year period (Thurgood and Weinman, 1991, p. 31). Among MBRS students earning doctorates of all kinds, 56.7 percent were African American and 65.1 percent were male (National Institutes of Health, 1992).

Interviews with current undergraduate MBRS students, as well as with doctorate holders now in teaching and research careers, make clear that MBRS and MARC program support plays a critical role in the development of minority scientists. "I know I'm going to get a Ph.D.," says undergraduate Marjorie Bonhomme. "I don't want to be a lab technician. I want to be in control of the project." Looking back at the path that took her from Jackson State to the Ohio State University College of Dentistry, Dr. Freddie Jordan says that MBRS "just opened the door. I didn't have any support system, growing up in the country. There aren't a lot of Ph.D.'s. So it put me in that environment. . . . If I had not been exposed to MBRS, I wouldn't be sitting where I am today." Program participants do not underestimate the significance of financial support: "I would have wound up with loans up to my neck, if I could even get them," Dr. Jordan remarks. But most comments dwell on the human support and the early chance to *do* real scientific research with a mentor in the laboratory.

A Sense of Belonging Rather than Isolation

The MBRS/MARC student's sense of purpose and close working relationship with faculty and fellow students stand in sharp contrast to the experience of many minority students on predominantly White campuses. A number of studies have documented the isolation and, ultimately, depression felt by minority students who now come increasingly from the inner city (Allen and Haniff, 1991; Fleming, 1984; Mestre, 1986; Saufley, Cowan, and Blake, 1983). The situation can be particularly devastating for minority males on White campuses. Fleming (1984) contrasts the withdrawal and loss of energy of African American males, especially in the senior year, at White campuses, with their vitality and higher motivation at traditional Black campuses. A minority student at Old Westbury, not in MBRS, describes his version of a common classroom experience: "People in my classes are predominantly White. I'm the only Black male, with maybe one or two of the sisters. I have to prove myself. I automatically feel like, wow, I have to say something slick to let them know that I'm just as cultured if not more. I'm a proud Black man and I walk in holding my head up, looking at everybody and I go to my seat. I try to be humble, but then they're all laughing and raising their hands and I sit back and then I walk out." The obvious conflict between this student's need "to prove myself" and his lack of an opportunity to do so beyond holding his head high can only lead to frustration. MBRS student Marjorie Bonhomme contrasts her clear sense of direction with what she sees of students in other areas: "Most students come to college with a lot of energy, but they have no direction and they just pick the easy courses where they will get an A. After a few semesters of this they get scared and lose all their energy because they don't see themselves going anywhere."

For many minority students, predominantly White institutions, with their academic emphasis on analysis, competition, and independent work, are an alien environment compared to the more relational, cooperative home cultures they come from (Hale-Benson, 1986). For Native Americans, for example, competition conflicts with Indian cultural values and Indian students often give up in the face of the competitive, aggressive atmosphere of White schools (O'Brien, 1990). Tribal colleges, despite impoverished conditions, by contrast show remarkable success because they are organized around Indian values. For Hispanic students, the additional complication of a lack of English language competency is often a further alienating factor. A series of studies of Hispanic science and engineering students reveals, for example, that certain Spanish language constructions, such as a difference in the meaning of double negatives, may interfere in English with the kind of logical reasoning essential to solving mathematics problems (Mestre, 1986).

A Formula for Success in Science Education

The experiences related by participants suggest that the MBRS and MARC programs over the past twenty years have pioneered strategies for moving minorities into science careers. These same strategies—mentoring, hands-on research, role models, collaboration rather than competition, and financial support—are now recognized as the essential ingredients in science education for all students. Project Kaleidoscope, a National Science Foundation–sponsored study of undergraduate science and mathematics, attributes the remarkable success of historically black and women's colleges in turning out science graduates to three factors: close relations between students and faculty, the presence of clear role models, and a critical mass of students from a particular group, which in the case of women, it can be argued, is optimally classes consisting entirely of women. A "talent development" approach rather than "talent sifting" characterizes these institutions. Project Kaleidoscope (1991b, p. 64) describes this attitude toward students as "cultivation" rather than "weeding," and "pumping" rather than "filtering."

It is not surprising, then, that seventeen of the top twenty institutions ranked according to baccalaureate origins of African American Ph.D's are HBCU's. And only two of these top twenty schools had neither an MBRS nor MARC program. Along the same lines, the University of Puerto Rico at Rio

Piedras and Mayaguez (both MBRS institutions) produce almost ten times more Hispanic baccalaureate holders who go on to receive doctorates than the third-place University of Texas (Thurgood and Weinman, 1991, p. 45). Similarly, far more women baccalaureates in the sciences from women's colleges proceed to earn doctorates than do those from coeducational schools (Sebrechts, 1992, p. 24).

Applying the Concept Across the Academic Disciplines

What would it take to replicate the successful features of the MBRS and MARC programs across the disciplines, in the humanities and social sciences, and in professional and preprofessional areas? We might begin by challenging national funding agencies to support undergraduate faculty research and the requisite accompanying student research assistantships. Students would start to see how the hands-on research and writing they are doing under the direction of a mentor could be developed into a professional career. And faculty would find that the experience of working with students on a research project would carry over into the classroom in a more realistic expectation of student accomplishments.

An MBRS student, however, was savvy enough to point out the unlikelihood of such funding: "The government only funds what they think is important. They do not see that art and the humanities will put money back in their pocket. We must show them this will educate our society and convince them." Some successful pilot projects modeled on MBRS might convince foundations, if not government agencies, that involvement in genuine research has the best chance of starting a minority undergraduate on the path to the professoriate. Given the sobering prospect that some half a million faculty positions overall must be filled between 1995 and 2010 (Schuster, 1989, p. 96), evidence of a project that jump-starts undergraduate research interest, especially among minorities, should be very persuasive.

Faculty and administrators must be inventive in finding ways to encourage the kind of mentoring that is based on a solid academic working relationship rather than on the good will of some faculty members, no matter the match of academic interests. Blackwell (1989) describes how complex and important this kind of mentoring can be at the undergraduate and graduate levels, and between junior and senior faculty. His prescriptions for mentors—including students in research, challenging them, providing support and encouragement, socializing them in the "role requirements" of the profession, and so on—are all familiar from MBRS and MARC. To stimulate mentoring of undergraduates, students can be given limited academic credit as a reward for entering a mentoring relationship, and faculty could be encouraged to guide students by tying faculty research grants to a requirement to enlist student assistants. More professional associations could follow the lead of the National Conferences on Undergraduate Research, which annually sponsors a conference where undergraduates in several disciplines, attending with faculty advisers, present papers and discuss national issues. It would also be valuable for minority organizations within the larger professional associations to assure that minority students can come together with their academic peers in a regional or national setting. A semester or a year "abroad" at an HBCU, tribal, or women's college, or at a branch of the University of Puerto Rico, might also give minority students that larger sense of identification by group or gender that helps motivation.

A subtle but essential element underlying the success of the MBRS/MARC student-faculty relationship is a kind of mutual respect where the faculty member neither coddles nor dominates the student. Scientists, it seems, find it natural to give student assistants a good deal of independence, while at the same time enforcing strict expectations about the work at hand. The very nature of modern scientific research is built on this openness to new approaches and the primacy of what can be presently verified, often by a research team working together. The typical experience in humanities research, however, is quite different: work is mostly solitary and based to a large degree on the authority of the text and an accumulated body of critical opinion. This situation may be changing, as the lively arguments over reader-based interpretation and the social construction of knowledge suggest. But faculty outside the sciences must seek inventive ways to involve students in research; they must guard against their inclination to "profess" with student research assistants or to assign them busywork rather than treating them as true collaborators.

Recruiting and Nurturing Minority Faculty

While the MBRS and MARC programs are making an impact, at their current levels of funding they alone cannot effectively address the shortage of minority scientists, including scientists in the professoriate. Increased funding for these and similar programs is certainly warranted, but must also be accompanied by changes in the ways that minority scientists are socialized into their disciplines and work places. Particularly troubling, for example, is the tenuous position of several of the interviewees for this chapter who have already run the gauntlet of science education, completed doctorates, and been hired to teach and/or do research. In spite of their accomplishments, they tend to be in untenured positions. One interviewee described his condition in these words: "This is purgatory, the twilight zone. . . . I'm in a Catch-22. Not having a lab of my own or being on a tenure track, I'm having trouble getting my own grants."

The notion that there is heavy competition for a limited pool of minority faculty candidates in the sciences is often used as an excuse for failing to conduct a vigorous search, but it may be more myth than reality. Evidence shows that minorities, especially African Americans and Native Americans, are more often underutilized or even unemployed, and if hired are let go sooner than other faculty (Carter and Wilson, 1992).

Academic institutions that hire talented minority faculty must also avoid the pitfalls of assigning high teaching loads which stifle creativity, and of asking junior faculty to assume duties that are essentially administrative too early in their careers. It is too often simply taken for granted that minority faculty should accept the time-consuming task of academic and personal counseling of all minority students. In addition, care should be taken to avoid burdening these faculty with multiple committee assignments in an effort to achieve minority representation on these committees. Most important, junior-level minority faculty must be mentored by a senior colleague who will advise them, provide them with information, and monitor their progress and development. Trust must be established so that frank and open discussion occurs, and the department should ensure that the individual is included in its social and academic life, such as meetings, colloquia, and seminars. To ensure the vitality of the pipeline, a similar mentoring system for new minority graduate students by a more senior counterpart is appropriate.

Summary

The MBRS and MARC programs are making a significant contribution to developing minority biomedical scientists, many of whom will pursue careers in academia. The essential element of these programs is the close research collaboration between students and faculty that helps to develop skills and engenders self-confidence critical to academic and personal success. An MBRS/MARC approach to education, based on a mentoring role anchored firmly in academic work, is good for all students. But it is more important the more removed a student's previous experience is from the academic world, and this is the case for many minority students now coming to college. As these students move up the academic career ladder, institutions have a responsibility to create an environment conducive to the development and growth of minority graduate students and faculty. Every faculty member can apply MBRS/MARC principles. The reward will come when faculty members can have students say about a shared research experience what Karlene Bryson said after first complaining about how exacting scientific research is: "But when I walk away from that lab, I am going to be able to say to myself, 'You know what, I can do it, it's nothing.' "

References

Allen, W. R., and Haniff, N. Z. "Race, Gender, and Academic Performance in U.S. Higher Education." In W. R. Allen, E. G. Epps, and N. Z. Haniff (eds.), *College in Black and White.* Albany: State University of New York Press, 1991.

Blackwell, J. E. "Mentoring: An Action Strategy for Increasing Minority Faculty." *Academe,* 1989, 75 (5), 8–14.

Carter, D. J., and Wilson, R. *1991 Tenth Annual Status Report on Minorities in Higher Education.* Washington, D.C.: American Council on Education, 1992.

Fleming, J. *Blacks in College: A Comparative Study of Students' Success in Black and in White Institutions.* San Francisco: Jossey-Bass, 1984.

Garrison, H. H., and Brown, P. W. *Minority Access to Research Careers: An Evaluation of the Honors Undergraduate Research Training Program.* Washington, D.C.: National Academy Press, 1985.

Hale-Benson, J. E. *Black Children: Their Roots, Culture, and Learning Styles.* (rev. ed.) Baltimore: Johns Hopkins University Press, 1986.

Mestre, J. P. "The Latino Science and Engineering Student: Recent Research Findings." In M. A. Olivas (ed.), *Latino College Students.* New York: Teachers College Press, 1986.

National Institutes of Health. Data provided by staff of the National Institute of General Medical Sciences and the Division of Research Resources. Bethesda, Md., June 1992.

O'Brien, E. M. "A Foot in Each World: American Indians Striving to Succeed in Higher Education." *Black Issues in Higher Education,* 1990, 7 (2), 27–31.

Project Kaleidoscope. *What Works: Building Natural Science Communities.* Washington, D.C.: Stamats Communications, 1991a.

Project Kaleidoscope. *What Works: Resources for Reform.* Washington, D.C.: Stamats Communications, 1991b.

Saufley, R. W., Cowan, K. O., and Blake, J. H. "The Struggles of Minority Students at Predominantly White Institutions." In J. H. Cones, III, J. F. Noonan, and D. Janha (eds.), *Teaching Minority Students.* New Directions for Teaching and Learning, no. 16. San Francisco: Jossey-Bass, 1983.

Schuster, J. H. "The Unmaking of the Black Professoriate: Context, Analysis, Proposal." In J. C. Elam (ed.), *Blacks in Higher Education: Overcoming the Odds.* Lanham, Md.: University Press of America, 1989.

Sebrechts, J. S. "The Cultivation of Scientists at Women's Colleges." *Journal of NIH Research,* 1992, 4 (6), 22–26.

Solmon, L. C., and Wingard, T. L. "The Changing Demographics: Problems and Opportunities." In P. G. Altbach and K. Lomotey (eds.), *The Racial Crisis in American Higher Education.* Albany: State University of New York Press, 1991.

Thurgood, D. H., and Weinman, J. M. *Summary Report 1990: Doctorate Recipients from United States Universities.* Washington, D.C.: National Academy Press, 1991.

ROBERT M. HOYTE *is Distinguished Teaching Professor in the Chemistry Department and director of the Minority Biomedical Research Support program at the State University of New York, College at Old Westbury.*

JONATHAN COLLETT *is professor in the Comparative Humanities Program and faculty coordinator of the Teaching for Learning Center at the State University of New York, College at Old Westbury.*

A writing support group helps women faculty maintain scholarly productivity in the face of multiple, often conflicting demands on their time, and it develops their sense of identity as writers.

A Writing Support Program for Junior Women Faculty

Joanne Gainen

Although graduate study provides an apprenticeship in doing research, many newly hired faculty find that the conditions for scholarly productivity are new and surprisingly demanding. Even at teaching-oriented institutions such as my own, new faculty are increasingly expected to publish in good journals while teaching six or more courses each year and becoming contributing members of their department and the larger institution.

The difficulty of meeting these challenging expectations is often exacerbated for women and minorities. Frequently, they begin their faculty careers without having experienced the advantages of rich graduate-school mentoring experiences equivalent to those of White males (Turner, Thompson, and Louis, in press). As faculty members, women and minorities continue to receive less mentoring and guidance than their White male colleagues (Boice, in press). Moreover, faculty of color may find few colleagues of similar ethnicity either for collegial interaction or to help meet the demand for female or minority representation on committees or in mentoring roles. Compounding the challenges they face, some of these new recruits encounter environments that are overtly hostile, racist, sexist, or combative (Blum, 1991; Brush, 1991). Not surprisingly, then, newly hired women and minority faculty may find themselves hard pressed to accomplish their scholarly agendas during the pretenure years.

This chapter describes a program to help new and junior faculty members accomplish scholarly writing while developing a balance of personal and professional activities. After describing the writing support program, I outline some of the issues we have discussed and strategies that have enabled participants to advance their scholarship and (as we have discovered) enhance their sense of identity and community as writers. While the program was not originally designed for women faculty, it is they who have taken advantage of it and made it their own.

Campus Context

Santa Clara University is a comprehensive Jesuit university with a strong liberal arts tradition; faculty are expected to be excellent teachers and scholars as well as collegial academic citizens. Internal funds support some research and curricular development but the majority of scholarship must be completed while teaching two courses per quarter, usually unaided by teaching or research assistants. An unspoken traditional "open-door" policy of availability to students limits uninterrupted time for scholarly research and writing. Moreover, women face an additional challenge: a recent study on our campus revealed that students expect significantly greater accessibility and supportiveness from women faculty as compared to their male counterparts (Bachen, McLoughlin, and Garcia, 1992). These conditions help to explain why one new faculty member described her first four weeks on campus as "overwhelming," another said she was "frantic," while a third—in her second year and not an inexperienced teacher—described herself as "exhausted with teaching." In such a climate, as one junior faculty woman stated, "It is difficult to keep scholarly writing central."

Fortunately, women at Santa Clara have a tradition of both informal and organized peer support. Since 1981, a strong women's studies program has increased women's presence on campus, provided an intellectual home for feminist scholars, and celebrated women's accomplishments at an annual dinner. "Kids on Campus," a childcare program founded by a woman faculty member (who herself had no children), serves both faculty and staff parents, although the length of its waiting list is legendary. In recent years women at Santa Clara have established an extensive support network, the Women Faculty Group, that addresses concerns of women faculty through programs, advocacy, and a newsletter. Until recently, however, no formal programs existed to support the development of women or minority faculty as scholars.

Origins of the Writing Group

In December 1989 the Teaching and Learning Center sponsored a discussion of Aisenberg and Harrington's *Women of Academe: Outsiders in the Sacred Grove* (1988). Although held on the last Friday of fall quarter, the session drew nearly forty faculty members, mostly women, many untenured. The book, summarized for busy participants in a review (Bell, 1989), had a tremendous impact as women faculty realized that they were not alone in their difficulties with scholarly productivity and acceptance. The discussion led to formation of the Women Faculty Group (mentioned above) and the initiation of Teaching and Learning Center programs to help faculty (both women *and* men) increase their sense of control related to issues of scholarly productivity. The writing support group grew out of the latter programs.

Our formal discussions of scholarly productivity and balance issues began at an annual midwinter retreat in 1991; junior faculty were especially encouraged to attend. To prepare for the retreat, participants maintained a time log for three days; at the retreat, we categorized our activities in terms of urgency and importance (Covey, 1989). Our analysis revealed what many had sensed: much of our time was spent in "urgent and important" activities, driven by deadlines and crises. Very little time was spent in "important but not urgent" time use such as planning, recreation, and exercise. The retreat continued with discussion of ways to be more efficient and effective in teaching and to make time during the school year for brief writing sessions.

At participants' request the retreat was followed in spring term by a three-hour workshop on scholarly productivity, this time presented by Robert Boice. Again, the program was scheduled at the end of a busy quarter, but twenty-one new and junior faculty attended—perhaps lured by the promise of a free copy of *Professors as Writers* (Boice, 1990). In the workshop Boice compared the writing and class preparation strategies of more- and less-successful faculty categorized on the basis of their teaching effectiveness. Effective teachers in his study spent *less* time preparing for class than their not-so-successful counterparts, who often overprepared for lectures, leaving little time for student interaction. Interestingly, more-successful teachers also wrote *more* regularly and indulged less often in "binge" writing, resulting in greater productivity with lower stress. Successful teachers, whom Boice labeled "quick starters," also spent more time in collegial interaction and had more-positive attitudes toward students and faculty. Although these findings do not demonstrate that reducing class preparation time will lead to better teaching and greater productivity, a group of less-successful faculty who adopted the work patterns of "quick starters" did seem to find greater success in both scholarship and teaching (Boice, 1992b).

The winter retreat and Boice's workshop generated both interest and skepticism among participants and their colleagues who learned about it through the "grapevine." Again based on participants' suggestions, I convened the first writing group session within a month after the workshop, and news of the group spread rapidly. Our numbers quickly expanded from six to about twelve, too large to conduct meetings effectively within our one-hour limit, so a second group was formed in early fall. Although all participants in the workshop were invited, only women actually signed up for the group meetings.

What Do We Do in These Meetings?

The concept of the group is simple: I schedule meetings twice per month at which we discuss our progress on scholarly writing projects, obstacles and strategies for overcoming them, and plans for the future. A central organizing theme for our work is that writing is most enjoyable and productive when completed in brief, daily sessions on work days throughout the academic year. Each of the participants seeks, in different ways, to minimize the need for writing "binges" by making writing a regular part of her weekly schedule. We also discuss social skills and collegial practices related to scholarly productivity. Our discussions integrate research on scholarly productivity with the collective wisdom of the group.

To model the important skill of setting limits, we try to limit meetings to one hour. At each meeting we take turns discussing the status of our writing projects, any obstacles we are facing, and both immediate and long-range plans. I serve as facilitator and "coach," although everyone provides suggestions; when time permits, I report on my progress as well.

As facilitator, I introduce an "agenda item" to stimulate discussion approximately once each quarter. For example, in our early meetings, we completed a writing questionnaire to assess possible writing blocks (Boice, 1990). During winter quarter I distributed a checklist entitled "Are You Solving the Right Problems?" based on factors that differentiate more-successful from less-successful women and minority faculty (Boice, in press). In spring, we discussed an article that relates writing strengths and weaknesses to personality characteristics assessed on the Myers-Briggs Type Inventory (Jensen and DiTiberio, 1984).

Each of us tries to leave each meeting with a clear plan for the next two weeks' writing tasks, and we report at the next meeting how well we lived up to our plan. We also troubleshoot, assessing each other's strategies for approaching writing tasks and occasionally discussing ways to reduce time spent on other activities (such as grading papers or taking on minor but time-consuming assignments for the department). Occasionally we role-play social skills related to writing and time management (for example, declining a chair's request to coordinate a conference) and we discuss strategies for dealing with writing blocks. We generally do not discuss the content of participants' work other than to identify which of several projects the speaker is referring to.

Not all members attend all meetings, so we now hold just two monthly meetings. We have found that with four or five participants we can usually discuss each person's situation in some detail and still finish within our one-hour time limit. We are not always that efficient or precise in allotting "airtime," but over time we generally manage to address the concerns of most participants.

Issues

Several themes emerged in our discussions. We focused most often on (1) identifying and dealing with writing blocks and fears of rejection, (2) establishing a regular time for writing and carrying out the schedule, (3) setting limits, and (4) professional decision making.

Dealing with Writing Blocks. Using Boice's (1990) writing attitudes questionnaire, members identified issues ranging from procrastination and fear of rejection to perfectionism. Several group members noticed that they became very enthusiastic when preparing and presenting conference papers but lost energy and began to doubt the value or originality of their ideas when preparing to write for journal publication. To counteract this negative "self-talk," we exchanged examples of *positive* self-talk (for example, "You will feel great when this is done"). We also discussed the importance of setting realistic, manageable goals for writing projects, and breaking the project into very small tasks. At this stage too members found it reassuring to learn that the average number of rejections before a paper is published is estimated to be about 3.5. They liked the idea that "rejection is normal." One member took a significant step toward dealing with rejection when she wrote to an editor, asking him to give specific reasons why her manuscript had been rejected. Another claims to have developed a "tougher skin," overcoming some "deflating experiences with manuscript rejection over the years." She now seeks early feedback on drafts and is determined to develop "staying power" with her manuscripts.

Establishing and Maintaining a Regular Writing Schedule. Most of the participants have established a schedule of desired writing times; maintaining these ideal schedules remains a challenge. Writing in the morning before becoming absorbed in the day's tasks is a strategy often recommended, but for many women family responsibilities make a morning schedule impractical. Several of our members schedule classes to free two or three days a week for writing. Even so, class preparation, meetings with students, trips to the library, and departmental or committee meetings often lure us away from writing on these days. Some members also faced significant difficulties related to availability of computer equipment and support.

We have all struggled to get writing done according to our schedules. One member, skeptical about the idea of a writing regimen, decided to "observe what happens when I write in the morning." (Six months later at a birthday luncheon she gave vivid testimonial to the joys of this practice.) Several members were able to maintain writing schedules for the first part of a quarter but found they had to abandon them as the pressures of exams and student papers accelerated. Some of our members have found they can use brief irregular times during the week to accomplish writing. One member established a Monday-Wednesday-Friday schedule and stuck to it religiously during fall quarter. At our final spring quarter meeting she proudly displayed the published version of her paper to cheers and applause from the group.

The most common pattern remains one of irregular adherence to a planned schedule, supplemented by extended evening and weekend writing sessions, particularly when a deadline looms. Nonetheless, several members of the group have established rigorous schedules and are sticking to them. One member, who originally felt she could not write at home, now regularly works at home two days per week. "I don't think I would have the forceful commitment to this strategy without the writing support group," she says. Another comments, "The group strengthened my resolve that it doesn't work to rely on summers alone—there isn't sufficient time then and I dislike the intense pressure from placing all my plans and hopes in one block of time. I benefited from hearing other people's stories and strategies about how to manage writing time during the academic year."

Setting Limits, Saying No. Involvement in the life of the institution is an important component of success and satisfaction for new faculty (Boice, 1992a). However, the seductiveness of such opportunities and the desire to please those who offer them can derail new faculty if they fail to recognize the extent to which committee work can intrude upon their time. Writing group members struggle to establish priorities and limit their involvement in these activities; when they could not take advantage of valued opportunities, they felt both frustration and guilt at refusing a colleague or administrator. Discussion of these issues at one meeting led to a spontaneous role-play in which one member excused herself from serving on a committee while others coached her "performance." She later did step down from the committee, and now stays informed and offers input through a colleague. Following the advice of a senior faculty member, I now advise junior faculty to dedicate their service efforts to one key committee relevant to their deepest concerns.

Saying no to students is just as challenging as declining an invitation from the department chair or a valued senior colleague. As I indicated earlier, students at Santa Clara expect faculty, especially women faculty, to be available and accessible to them. One member of the group was astonished to find that students continued to knock on her door even when she posted a sign saying "Sacred writing time. Please do not disturb." We frequently discussed the importance of notifying the department chair of writing plans and schedules and enlisting the chair's cooperation in rerouting or rescheduling students. Nonetheless, for many of us the most viable strategy remains working at home.

Another source of stress and consternation is grading. More than one of our members has found herself "buried" under stacks of papers to be graded. All of us view writing as an integral part of the learning process; members are not willing to relinquish what they see as their responsibility to assign writing and provide thoughtful feedback on students' work. At our sessions we periodically discuss ways to make writing assignments and feedback strategies more efficient to create more time for our own writing. One approach we discussed is to let students give each other feedback during the early stages of writing, so that the final version would be of higher quality and (theoretically) easier to grade. Participants also experimented with different forms of assignments—for example, asking students to list key ideas on a topic rather than having them write an essay exam. One member reduced the number of writing assignments, but later felt that students were coming to class less prepared on nonwriting days than when writing assignments were due. Another group member tried having students grade quizzes in class before returning them to her. In spite of these and other innovations, giving feedback on papers and grading essay exams remain major "time grabbers" for most of the group.

Professional Decision Making. Throughout the year members of the group assisted each other in making decisions about how to allocate writing time. As the year progressed we realized that many of our publication projects were derailed by the need to prepare conference papers on a different subject. The deadlines and social expectations imposed by conference papers spurred much "binge" writing, but as we reviewed our accomplishments we found that we rarely fulfilled our plans to turn conference papers into publication-quality manuscripts. In addition, we observed that we often missed out on the networking opportunities afforded by conference attendance because we were working on last-minute revisions of our papers. We dubbed this cluster of busyness symptoms the "conference paper syndrome."

As a result of our observations, several group members have decided to limit the number of conference proposals they submit to perhaps one or two per year, and have made specific plans to turn at least one paper into a publishable manuscript. We have also discussed ways to profit from networking opportunities available at conferences, for example, by arranging, prior to a conference, meetings with people we want to see.

Our conversations about career planning and decision making revealed ambivalence about goals of professional visibility. In discussing the handout mentioned earlier, "Solving the Right Problems," several group members objected that successful male faculty members' goals of "visibility and portability" implied exploitation of the faculty member's home institution. In voicing their responsibility to students and to the institution, they failed to realize the importance of external collegial networks for their own professional development. Perhaps this view helps to explain why members of the group tend to have a relatively limited set of external colleagues or mentors with whom to exchange work in progress. In addition to fostering a sense of professional invisibility and isolation, the lack of such ties limits women's development as scholars and can be problematic when they suggest external reviewers for tenure committees.

Impact of the Writing Group

The group's impact can be assessed in terms of its role in helping participants achieve writing goals and its influence on our perceptions of ourselves as writers.

Achievements of Writing Group Members. Each of the twelve faculty women associated with the group presented at least one conference paper during the academic year; the modal number was two, and one person presented four. Everyone also had at least one manuscript in progress intended for a refereed journal, often based on a conference paper. Four of the ten regular members of the group completed manuscripts and submitted them to refereed journals during the year. Three had articles accepted, and one received a book contract. Two received rejections during the year but resubmitted the manuscripts after making minor changes. While it is difficult to obtain comparative data, participants generally acknowledge the group's importance in helping them achieve these results.

Perception of Self as Writer. In addition to making progress in their writing, participants have repeatedly affirmed another important function of the group: it has helped them to develop their identity as scholarly writers. As one member noted, "We spend most of our time on teaching. One good effect of the writing group is that we think about this other 'hat' we wear as writers. . . . The underlying message [of the group] is that we are writers— and we ought to attend to that. When I'm writing I feel fine. When I'm not writing, I'm not right with the world. I'm failing. I'm not living up to my responsibility to myself."

In a recent meeting another member observed that she is "learning how a scholar works . . . we need criticism." This understanding, and her increased confidence in her judgment as a writer, enabled her to share a draft manuscript with a colleague for the first time. And in finishing her latest manuscript she began to see her first book developing naturally out of her current work. One member has begun to keep records of her writing time and enjoys watching her accomplishments add up. Another member still struggles to find time for writing; during the summer, when writing regularly, she "felt on track with all aspects of my being." Now facing new responsibilities, she experiences *not* writing as "a huge guilty secret" that "makes it hard to feel good about other accomplishments." Her goal this year: to build up a "small practice" of writing in fifteen-minute periods each day.

Not all those who initially signed up for the group found that it met their needs. Two did not continue because they wanted to exchange and discuss

actual manuscripts; and one first-year faculty member who had not participated in either of the two introductory programs felt the group was not
helpful to her in her writing, although it was valuable for meeting people.
The program also did not reach some faculty who probably could have
benefitted.

Spinoffs. One unexpected way in which group members have pursued
their developing identities as writers is by creating writing partnerships
outside the group. At least two such partnerships have formed in recent
months; partners meet periodically over lunch, talk on the telephone, or
correspond by e-mail to report on their progress between group meetings.
Partners report that these valuable and enjoyable discussions deepen and
extend the work of the group. In addition, word of the groups' success has
traveled around campus with the result that one department chair plans to
establish a departmental writing group. Several senior faculty members have
also expressed interest in the program. Finally, my role as facilitator and
participant has lent momentum to my own writing projects and increased
my understanding of issues faced by junior faculty related to writing as well
as teaching.

Implications

My observations of the group's natural history and my experiences as both
facilitator and participant underscore for me a point often overlooked in the
design of faculty development programs: the kinds of changes we seek to
induce (whether about writing habits or teaching styles) may require several
years of sustained practice and support during periods of occasional back-
sliding. In workshops and retreats we can introduce junior faculty to
productivity strategies used by successful colleagues. But like many individuals seeking to change long-standing habits, junior faculty also benefit
from structured social supports to develop and maintain new work patterns.
In casual conversations around the department, these faculty may pick up
ideas and helpful hints to improve their situation, and some may be
fortunate to find a mentor within the institution. Participating in a writing
group, though, improves the odds that help will be forthcoming. It legiti-
mizes and creates occasions for frequent, in-depth, confidential, and supportive discussion of each participant's involvement in writing. Few
departments or campuses provide such informal yet systematic, sustained
support to communicate the tacit knowledge of scholarship to the next
generation of faculty.

The writing support group does more than help junior women faculty
find time for writing. For these "outsiders in the sacred grove," the simple
experience of sharing writing conflicts and celebrating both large and small
successes may serve to quell self-doubts and strengthen hard-won but
sometimes fragile professional identities. And although these groups repre-

sent a small institutional investment, they offer promise as a way to strengthen the collegial ties that are so important to a new faculty member's success.

References

Aisenberg, N., and Harrington, M. *Women of Academe: Outsiders in the Sacred Grove.* Amherst: University of Massachusetts Press, 1988.

Bachen, C., McLoughlin, M., and Garcia, S. "Gender in the Classroom: Observations and Strategies." Presentation to the Women Faculty Group, Santa Clara University, Apr. 21, 1992.

Bell, C. "Little Men: Review of *Women of Academe.*" Unpublished manuscript, Santa Clara University, 1989.

Blum, D. E. "Environment Still Hostile to Women in Academe, New Evidence Indicates." *Chronicle of Higher Education,* Oct. 9, 1991, pp. A1, A20.

Boice, R. *Professors as Writers.* Stillwater, Okla.: New Forums Press, 1990.

Boice, R. *The New Faculty Member.* San Francisco: Jossey-Bass, 1992a.

Boice, R. "What Can We Learn from Quick Starters?" In M. Theall and J. Franklin (eds.), *Effective Practices for Improving Teaching.* New Directions for Teaching and Learning, no. 48. San Francisco: Jossey-Bass, 1992b.

Boice, R. "New Faculty Involvement of Women and Minorities." *Research in Higher Education,* in press.

Brush, S. G. "Women in Science and Engineering." *American Scientist,* 1991, 79, 404–419.

Covey, S. R. *The Seven Habits of Highly Effective People.* New York: Simon & Schuster, 1989.

Jensen, G. H., and DiTiberio, J. K. "Personality and Individual Writing Processes." *College Composition and Communication,* 1984, 35 (3), 285–300.

Turner, C.S.V., Thompson, J. R., and Louis, K. S. "Minority Women Doctoral Students: An Examination of Socialization Experiences." In L. Welsh (ed.), *Perspectives on Minority Women in Higher Education.* New York: Greenwood/Praeger, in press.

JOANNE GAINEN (formerly Joanne Kurfiss) is director of the Teaching and Learning Center and associate dean for instruction and evaluation, College of Arts and Sciences, Santa Clara University, California.

CONCLUSION

In these pages we have surveyed demographic data and listened to the diverse voices of our nontraditional colleagues in an effort to understand the academic world from their point of view. We have seen clear evidence that while many critics would claim affirmative action has "done enough," in fact such efforts have barely made a dent in fostering greater diversity among the faculty at all ranks and in all institutional types. Moreover, in listening to our colleagues, we have been dismayed to hear of so many examples of overt and covert acts of discrimination and fundamental incivility. One implication that emerges from our inquiry, then, is that failing some dramatic changes of custom or significant external influences, many nontraditional groups will remain underrepresented in the academy even while their numbers increase in the population at large. Institutional practices that allow racism, sexism, homophobia, and other forms of prejudice to influence retention, graduate student assignments, promotion, tenure, and salary decisions are particularly onerous and must be confronted.

Failures of support at the undergraduate, graduate, and faculty level are the cause of much misery; in contrast, individuals who thrive (whether women, minorities, or traditional White males) universally report positive mentoring experiences such as those described by the exemplary junior faculty interviewed by Boice and the students in programs such as those described by Hoyte and Collett. Networks and support groups such as those described by Gainen may be equally powerful in helping women and minorities find community within the academy so that they will eventually take their places among its influential senior members. A second implication, then, is that mentoring and other forms of collegial interaction are essential features of a more supportive environment.

Building support networks and mentoring opportunities may help women and faculty of color succeed in the present system. But it is also necessary to examine critically the system itself. What has traditionally been defined as academic rigor requires scrutiny to the extent that new perspectives and approaches to scholarship and teaching are excluded simply because they are "different." Senior faculty, particularly those who serve on tenure and promotion committees, must educate themselves to recognize the value of nontraditional scholarship, teaching, and service. And they must confront discriminatory patterns like those revealed in the case of Don Nakanishi, whose lawyer reports that the reasons given for rejecting Nakanishi's prolific and "pathbreaking" (the committee's term) scholarship were identical to those given by a tenure committee in a similar case this lawyer had handled nearly a decade earlier (Minami, 1990). When we place all the responsibility on newcomers to adjust, accommodate, and sacrifice, we risk losing the intellectual vitality they have to offer. Regardless of demographic trends in the population as a whole, the faculty will remain relatively homogeneous unless those who hold power—the senior faculty and administrators who distribute recognition and rewards—radically alter their responses to the scholarship and values of nontraditional newcomers in our midst.

Each of the contributors to this volume helps make these points. Johnsrud's literature review leads her to conclude that academe sets vague criteria for tenure and promotion and offers outsiders less help than it grants to White males; she advocates training department chairs and senior faculty to support development of women and minority faculty in their pretenure years. Bronstein, Rothblum, and Solomon's depiction of "ivy halls and glass walls" reminds us that discouragement of women and people of color often begins in the primary and secondary school years and continues unabated through graduate education and beyond. Both Garza's and Bronstein's studies of nontraditional faculty, in turn, reveal a paradox in the current system: reflexive dismissal of outsiders' scholarship on issues of gender, ethnicity, and sexual orientation makes prospects of learning how to diversify professorial culture even more difficult. So too do public and private expressions of hostility toward those who differ from the current majority. With Tierney and Rhoads, Nakanishi reminds us that campus leaders must take an assertive and public role in both discouraging discrimination and in educating colleagues about the contributions that "communities of difference" can bring to the academy.

The final three chapters of this collection suggest where changes in the academy can most readily occur: in studies to help us understand early experiences of junior faculty that either integrate or exclude (Boice); in faculty mentoring that involves nontraditional students in the conversations of our disciplines, providing effective grounding and motivation for professorial and professional careers (Hoyte and Collett); and in attempts to implement simple but potentially significant programs of collegial support for activities such as scholarly productivity (Gainen).

Support programs such as these suggest directions for further research. To begin with, questions of effective faculty development practice merit immediate attention. For example, the diversity of issues and experiences reported in the chapters by Nakanishi, Garza, Tierney and Rhoads, and Boice suggest that the kinds of supports that will be most valuable in the long run may differ for different faculty groups. On the other hand, the common themes of devaluation and lack of collegial support and mentoring suggest areas for immediate attention independent of gender, ethnicity, or sexual orientation. Research on support programs is often neglected yet badly needed. For example, in preparing their manuscript for this collection, Robert Hoyte and Jonathan Collett discovered that in the nearly two decades the MBRS and MARC programs have been in existence (and federally funded), surprisingly little evaluation has been done. Methodologically, research on support programs must fully integrate the perspectives of program recipients both to improve program design and to deepen understanding of institutional practices that drive women and minorities out of the academy.

More fundamentally, however, we need better theoretical frameworks to understand sources of disenfranchisement of women and minorities and the ways in which institutions erect barriers to full participation for all. A critical perspective, such as that used to guide Tierney's (1992) investigation of educational experiences of Native Americans, can help us to understand how academic and cultural influences shape educational biographies toward or away from attainment of higher degrees. We need a better understanding of how race, class, gender, ethnicity, acculturation, and other dimensions of difference affect career paths in different kinds of academic environments. But we also need to understand the powerful social forces that work to exclude accomplished minority and women scholars from the top-ranked research universities, the highest academic ranks, and the most central administrative posts.

We recognize that the supportive efforts and systemic reassessment we propose imply significant changes in the attitudes and behaviors of many academics. Fortunately, we need not await large-scale social change, costly institutional funding, or government intervention to transform the academy, since the changes we advocate depend largely on the good will, open-mindedness, and compassion of academic leaders. For example, every faculty member and administrator who reads these accounts can take responsibility for enhancing the collegial environment in his or her domain; first steps might be as simple as conversing informally with new women and minority faculty about their needs and interests or as complex as formal self-studies such as those undertaken by Stanford University (All-University Forum on Diversity, 1992) or the University of Minnesota (University Committee on Minority Issues, 1989). Self-studies are an effective antidote to the common assertion that "we don't have those problems here," and they focus attention on areas of greatest need. Handbooks such as the American Council on Education's *Minorities on Campus: A Handbook for Enhancing Diversity* (Green, 1989) provide practical suggestions and policy recommendations to help address problems once they are identified.

On a personal level, each of us can make ourselves available to someone who is different from ourselves simply by initiating a supportive conversation on a regular basis. We can organize informal meetings to share our tacit understanding of institutional and departmental expectations. We can speak out when colleagues make inappropriate statements. Above all, we can educate ourselves to understand, respect, and reward the emerging intellectual perspectives offered by women and people of color.

In short, without having to label ourselves or our colleagues as "racist," "sexist," or "homophobic," we can all act in constructive ways to understand and reverse the patterns that separate traditional from nontraditional colleagues. Through reflection, dialogue, self-education, and constructive action, we can build the diverse faculty that will both reflect and shape the society of the future.

JOANNE GAINEN
ROBERT BOICE
EDITORS

References

All-University Forum on Diversity. *Report on the Self-Reflective Study: Attending to Human Details.* Minneapolis, MN: University of Minnesota, 1992.

Green, M. F. (ed.). *Minorities on Campus: A Handbook for Enhancing Diversity.* Washington, D.C.: American Council on Education, 1989.

Minami, D. "Guerilla War at UCLA: Political and Legal Dimensions of the Tenure Battle." *Amerasia Journal,* 1990, *16* (10), 81–107.

Tierney, W. G. *Official Encouragement, Institutional Discouragement: Minorities in Academe—The Native American Experience.* Norwood, N.J.: Ablex, 1992.

University Committee on Minority Issues. *Building a Multiracial, Multicultural University Community: Final Report of the University Committee on Minority Issues.* Palo Alto, Calif.: Stanford University, 1989.

ROBERT BOICE is professor of psychology and director of the Faculty Instructional Support Office at the State University of New York at Stony Brook. He is author of The New Faculty Member.

JOANNE GAINEN (formerly Joanne Kurfiss) is director of the Teaching and Learning Center and associate dean in the College of Arts and Sciences, Santa Clara University, California. She is author of Critical Thinking: Theory, Research, Practice, and Possibilities.

INDEX

Academe. *See* Higher education
Affirmative action, failure, 35–36
African Americans: doctorate degrees, 8, 82, 84–85, 87; early educational experiences, 18; primary academic activity, 8; scholarly productivity, 8. *See also* Minority faculty
Aisenberg, N., 7, 92
Allen, W. R., 85
Alpert, D., 4
American Association of University Women, 18, 23, 29
American Association of University Women Educational Foundation, 18, 21, 22
American Educational Research Association, 58
American Psychological Association, 58
Andrews, P. H., 6, 11
Appelbaum, D., 8
Armour, R., 6, 7, 12
Arnold, K. D., 21
Asian Pacific American faculty/administrators: action plan for, 57–58; and discrimination, 53–55; misconceptions about, 52–57; passivity vs. proaction, 55–57; tenure, 56–57; underrepresentation, 51, 52–53
Asian Pacific Americans, doctorate degrees, 82
Asian Pacific Americans in Higher Education, 58
Association for Women in Psychology (AWP), 61
Association of American Colleges, 29
Association of Asian American Studies, 58
Astin, H. S., 6, 10
Attorney General's Asian Pacific Islander Advisory Committee, 54, 56
Atwater, C. D., 6, 7, 8, 11
Austin, A. E., 10

Bachen, C., 92
Banks, W. M., 8, 9, 10
Barinaga, M., 17, 25
Bell, C., 92

Berglund, P., 8
Big Ten institutions, 4
Bjork, L. G., 5
Black, L., 18, 24, 25
Blackburn, R. T., 8, 72
Blackwell, J. E., 87
Blake, J. H., 85
Blum, D. E., 17, 18, 23, 71, 91
Boice, R., 7, 8, 11, 72, 73, 74, 75, 91, 93, 94, 96
Bourguignon, E., 6, 8, 9, 10, 11
Bowen, H. R., 4, 5, 36
Bronstein, P., 18, 24, 25, 61
Brown, P. W., 84
Brown, S. V., 8
Brush, S. G., 91

California Faculty Association, 35, 39
California Postsecondary Education Commission, 33
California State University at Fresno, 35
California State University (CSU) system, 33, 34
Career, nontraditional faculty: course (study), 61–70; maps, 72, 77–78; obstacles, 78; points-of-no-return, 74–77; turning-point experiences, 72–74; turning points (study), 71–78; and undergraduate science experiences, 81–89
Career maps, 72, 77–78
Carnegie Faculty Survey, 36
Carnegie Foundation for the Advancement of Teaching, 6
Carter, D. J., 82, 89
Chairpersons: selection/training, 11; support for minority/women faculty, 10–12
Chamberlain, M. K., 22
Chan, S., 53
Chicano/Latino faculty: and affirmative action failure, 35–36; *barrio*ization, 36–37; devaluation, 38–39; factors threatening, 35; and institutional change, 39–40; layoffs, 35; minority service, 39; perceptions/experiences, 37–38; and racism, 9; tenure, 35, 38–

Ordering Information

New Directions for Teaching and Learning is a series of paperback books that presents ideas and techniques for improving college teaching, based both on the practical expertise of seasoned instructors and on the latest research findings of educational and psychological researchers. Books in the series are published quarterly in Spring, Summer, Fall, and Winter and are available for purchase by subscription as well as by single copy.

Subscriptions for 1993 cost $45.00 for individuals (a savings of 20 percent over single-copy prices) and $60.00 for institutions, agencies, and libraries. Please do not send institutional checks for personal subscriptions. Standing orders are accepted.

Single copies cost $14.95 when payment accompanies order. (California, New Jersey, New York, and Washington, D.C., residents please include appropriate sales tax.) Billed orders will be charged postage and handling.

Discounts for quantity orders are available. Please write to the address below for information.

All orders must include either the name of an individual or an official purchase order number. Please submit your order as follows:
   Subscriptions: specify series and year subscription is to begin
   Single copies: include individual title code (such as TL1)

Mail all orders to:
   Jossey-Bass Publishers
   350 Sansome Street
   San Francisco, California 94104

For single-copy sales outside of the United States contact:
   Maxwell Macmillan International Publishing Group
   866 Third Avenue
   New York, New York 10022

For subscription sales outside of the United States, contact
   any international subscription agency or Jossey-Bass directly.